home at 7 dinner at 8

Sophie Wright

home at 7 dinner at 8

Sophie Wright

Photography by

Romas Foord

KYLE CATHIE LIMITED

Dedication

I would like to dedicate this book to my Mum. Thanks for everything Mum. I love you very much.

First published in Great Britain in 2011 by
Kyle Cathie Limited
23, Howland Street
London W1T 4AY
www.kylecathie.com

ISBN: 978 1 85626 862 2

A CIP catalogue record for this title is available from
the British Library

Text © Sophie Wright 2011
Photographs © Romas Foord 2011
Design © Kyle Cathie Limited 2011

Editor: Vicky Orchard
Design: Nicky Collings
Photography: Romas Foord
Styling: Polly Webb-Wilson
Copy editor: Emma Callery
Production: Sheila Smith and Nic Jones

Colour reproduction by Altaimage Ltd
Printed and bound in China by Toppan Leefung
Printing Ltd

Note on ingredients
All eggs are large unless otherwise stated.

Acknowledgements

This book has been an absolute pleasure to write, and since we came up with idea around the table in Kyle Cathie office, I've not been able to stop thinking of fun, quick and easy recipes that would suit the title of this fabulous book.
It's a book for all people from all walks of life, but I must admit that I kept a few very key people in mind whilst writing it (Carly, Rosie, Tom...).

My main aim with *Home at 7, Dinner at 8* was accessibility. I want this book to be a bible of yummy recipes that everyone can have a go at. And yes Hannah, I'm talking about YOU! Hannah, you are my working girl stencil for making this book work! Mainly because if you can do it...anyone can!! So thank you for always giving it a go, and for letting me watch you make potato custard soup. Definitely an experience. Dan, you know what I'm taking about!!

I really want to mention my Mum, Ann, who is such a special person. You have not only given me my passion for food and cooking but also the ability to put my mind to something and do it well.

A lot has changed in my life over the last year or so, and I can say that this has probably been the best year yet. I have had the praise, support and kindness from people that will be with me forever. Tom...of course no meal is complete without a touch of Pepper!! You have been a tower of strength to me, not just with the book, but with everything and I hope someday I can be as strong for you as you have for me.

Oliver Wright, my beautiful little brother…Olly, I hope one day, when you're old enough to read this that you learn something and don't just open a tin! I promise I'll always lend you a hand if you ever get stuck.

Dad, not much else I can say than you're not only an amazing father to me, but also to Oliver and you're my absolute role model. I'm very proud to be your daughter.

Finally I must give a huge thanks to everyone at Kyle Cathie who has allowed this book to happen: Vicky, you're a star of an editor and your patience and attention to detail must certainly be praised. Thank you for all your hard work. Nicky, genius as ever, you are an absolute pleasure. And Romas, I must say that every shoot day was fabulous and you made making this book such an enjoyable experience. The pictures are stunning! Well done all of you, I hope you all love it as much as I do.

I know there are so many of you I have left out, but as with *Easy Peasy*, all my lovely friends and family I want to thank you so much. I'm extremely lucky to have you all and I hope you enjoy reading my new book that I have loved writing so much.

MAKE LIFE EASY FOR YOURSELF

Being able to cook a simple dinner that is ready to eat within an hour of getting home is something that everyone craves. But sometimes cooking supper after a long day at work can seem like a tedious task. For me cooking should be enjoyable – a way of winding down at the end of the day, perhaps with a glass of wine and a bit of music, or chatting to a friend or partner about your day while making a delicious meal. Easy, tasty and fresh dishes that can be prepared quickly with little effort and without sacrificing on flavour.

This book has the answer: all recipes can be on the table in an hour or less (most in 30 minutes and under), are suitable for a variety of occasions and can be enjoyed by friends, family, adults and children alike. I want this book to be the hardworking professional's bible that you can scan through the night before and know what you're going to pick up from the supermarket on your way home. I'll introduce you to a few of my favourite time-saving cheats, just to take the strain off, give you some suggestions for storecupboard essentials, the basics you'll use over and over, and show how by having a few bits of the right equipment you can become so much more confident when it comes to cooking. I also plan on showing you, in Watching the Pennies, how you can make really great family dinners without breaking the bank. So many ingredients are available for us in the supermarkets that we often walk straight past the real bargains. I plan to help you open your eyes a bit.

I always tended to go for the more difficult option when cooking (no shortcuts). That's fine on the weekends when you might have time to spare, but honestly, who does during the week? I now know that it's absolutely fine to use a few things such as pre-prepared ingredients that make your life much easier in the long run and make cooking far less stressful and time consuming.

I really want to stress that cooking isn't about getting worried that you are missing a certain ingredient or you can't find what you need in the supermarket. Just go with what you have and take it easy. The minute you start to get stressed, the less enjoyable and relaxing your cooking time will be. Just have fun.

When cooking during the week, I've now changed my whole attitude. I do whatever I can think of that's tasty and can be cooked in quick time. I want to have time to enjoy relaxing or spending with my friends or family, not be dragged away from them by the cooking while they are unwinding in front of the television with a glass of something cold.

I know it's easy to call in for a takeaway, or walk down to your local for a bit of food, but I hope these recipes will not only make your mouth water, but will also inspire you to cook at home and enjoy a quicker, healthier and cheaper alternative. I have written this book to encourage you all that cooking something interesting and fast in an evening can be done – and with new and exciting recipes. Enjoy!

ESSENTIAL INGREDIENTS

These are just a handful of things that we can buy to make our lives so much easier when cooking during the week.

STORECUPBOARD

Fresh ready-made gnocchi, tortellini and ravioli – enable you to eat meals that would otherwise take hours to make, without sacrificing quality

Any type of dried or fresh pasta such as spaghetti, penne or fusilli

Instant noodles such as glass noodles, straight-to-wok, soba or instant noodles

Cooked microwavable rice – helps you save on cooking and washing up time

Pre-cooked lentils, either tinned or packets – save 20–25 minutes by buying pre-cooked packet lentils and lose none of the nutritional benefits

Infused oils such as chilli, basil, lemon, garlic, avocado or nut oils – add instant flavour to any dish

Vinegars: balsamic (reasonable quality), cider, white wine, red wine, rice wine – allow you to be far more creative in the kitchen and bring out real flavour in foods you might otherwise avoid

Ready-made stocks and stock cubes – a storecupboard must-have no kitchen can be without. You can also bulk freeze pre-made stocks to use when necessary

Dried herbs such as dried oregano, thyme, herbes de Provence

Spices and pre-mixed spice blends such as ground cumin, ground coriander, *ras el hanout*, garam masala – instantly jazz up a piece of fish, roasted veggies or chicken breast

Chilli flakes – use these when you don't have fresh chillies to add a little spice to a dish

Good-quality pestos and pastes – available from the refrigerated section and last a good week or so in the fridge

Sweet chilli sauce

Soy sauce – light and dark

Tinned tomatoes, paste and passatas – cheap, never go off and an occasional life-saver for a quick pasta dish when supplies are running low

Marinated artichokes in a jar or fresh from the deli section – a great ingredient to have when you fancy being a bit more creative

Sunblush tomatoes or jar of sun-dried (the best quality are available from the fresh deli section) – full of flavour as someone else has done all the hard work of preparing them for you

Jar of ready-roasted peppers and vegetables

Pre-picked pomegranate seeds – colourful and healthy they add a little punch to any exotic dish

Tinned beans and pulses such as cannellini beans, kidney beans, flageolet beans, borlotti beans, butter beans and chickpeas – saves the fuss of soaking them in water and provide a good source of cheap protein and way of bulking out dinners

Ready-chopped garlic, ginger and chilli

FRIDGE
Parmesan, Cheddar or Gruyère and any type of blue cheese
Cream cheese
Eggs – handy for a quick omelette or fritters
Lemons
Onions
Small selection of fresh herbs if possible

FREEZER
Berries such as mixed fruits, strawberries, blackberries, raspberries
Peas
Broad and soya beans
Spinach
Prawns
Lots of ice – handy for making drinks
Bay leaves, thyme and fresh chillies – keep really well in the freezer
Pre-prepared stocks – either bought or homemade

EQUIPMENT AND COOKING TECHNIQUES

Now that you have a nicely stocked kitchen I'm going to let you in on a few little secrets on how to prepare all these great dinners you are going to cook with ease. Cooking isn't rocket science. It's all about common sense. What would you think if I tried to cook a nice piece of fish in an old beaten-up pan or chop parsley with a blunt knife? Trust me; I see this time and time again while doing my rounds of cooking lessons.

Here's a list of a few things I think you must have in order to be able to get home at 7 and have dinner at 8. Some of you may read this little list and say, well, I've got all that. If that's the case then just skip this section. If not, get a pen and paper and start writing that shopping list!

A sharp knife Not a knife that is so big you can't use it, just a simple 30cm cook's knife that can be used for almost every task.

A small serrated knife These are great for preparing ingredients like cherry tomatoes and citrus fruits. I couldn't be without mine.

A blender of sorts I know that a lot of you will have a big old chunky blender hanging around at the back of a cupboard that hasn't seen the light of day since it came out the box, so I would advise getting yourself a little space-saving option that fits in even the smallest of drawers and gets used on a regular basis. These little blenders cost a maximum of £25 and trust me they are worth every penny. I use mine for everything from chopping chillies and garlic for curries to making a quick fresh pesto.

A good-quality non-stick pan. This will make all the difference when cooking even the simplest of meals. They are great for frying fish, chicken breasts and eggs and making quick stir-fries if you don't have a wok. A non-stick pan is also a healthier option as you have to use half the amount of oil when cooking as nothing will stick to it.

Sharp scissors Seems obvious, but scissors are great when it comes to time-saving for everything from quickly snipping herbs to removing the backbone from a chicken.

A fine grater There are many different options on the market for sharp, fine graters and they are brilliant for everything from grating Parmesan, garlic and ginger to zesting lemons.

A casserole pan with a lid A kitchen must-have.

I think if you have these few basic bits your whole view on cooking will change. These are really easy solutions to making your life just that little bit easier.

Finally, a few handy tips when it comes to cooking:

Before you start cooking a recipe, familiarise yourself with it. You don't have to learn it by heart, just have a vague idea of the steps and what's meant to be going on and when. This way you won't need to have your head buried in a book while slightly overcooking the onions! You'll also feel so much more confident with the idea of cooking it.

Prepare all the ingredients before you actually start cooking anything. This means any chopping or blending that needs to be done should be done before you even turn on the heat under a pan. Do this while your oven or grill is preheating. I promise this will save you time in the long run.

Don't over-stretch yourself when cooking for friends or family so you end up getting stressed out. Cooking should be a nice, relaxing experience when possible and also inventive. If something goes wrong, don't panic, it's probably still edible. None of us are perfect. If something goes wrong or doesn't taste right one of the following tricks might help:

Fresh herbs liven up even the blandest of dishes so try to keep a small variety in your fridge and use them whenever possible.

If you are using chillies and you've gone a bit overboard, try adding a squeeze of lemon or a spoonful of yogurt or double cream. That will usually calm down the spice a little.

Never cook green vegetables with a lid on the saucepan and make sure the water is rapidly boiling before you add them to ensure you don't overcook and waterlog your vegetables.

Lastly, I have experienced what I'm sure many of you struggle with – a small kitchen! So I understand how difficult it can be cooking for any more than two people in a limited space. I've really tried to take this into consideration when designing these recipes; I've tried to use as few pots and pans as possible and hopefully most of the washing up can go in the dishwasher. If you don't have one, then leave it for someone else – one of my biggest rules is that if I cook, then there's no way I'm clearing up!

Everyday

Most of us after a long day just want dinner on the table (or our knees) as quickly as possible, so your evening can start and you can finally relax. We want food that is quick, simple to prepare and easy to eat. I have filled this chapter with recipes that will become a tried-and-trusted part of your weekly meal menu. We all have favourites that we cook time and time again because we can virtually prepare them with our eyes closed and that's exactly what I've planned for with these dishes. It's really important to me that these recipes are as accessible as possible and, of course, easy to shop for. Nothing flash, just good, friendly food.

ROASTED GUINEA FOWL WITH CHICORY, FENNEL AND ORANGE

55
TOTAL

Preparation **15**
Cooking **40**
Serves **4**

It's always nice to have a little change from a roast chicken, and guinea fowl is the closest variation. It's the same-sized bird, so cooks in the same amount of time, but it has a meatier flavour than chicken and slightly darker meat. It's best to remove the legs and wings from the crown so it cooks quicker. It's really delicious with rustic roasted vegetables (I like to buy red chicory heads as they add a bit of colour) and a few herbs and spices. Give it a go – you may be surprised.

1 guinea fowl
2 fennel bulbs, trimmed and cut into thin
  slices
3–4 heads of chicory, halved lengthways
4 carrots, peeled and cut into sticks
2 large oranges

2 tablespoons maple syrup
1 tablespoon fennel seeds
1 tablespoon chopped thyme leaves
2 tablespoons olive oil
salt and freshly ground black pepper

1 Preheat the oven to 190°C/375°F/Gas 5. Remove the legs from the guinea fowl by pulling them away from the carcass and cutting the skin that holds the legs to the body. Pull each leg back on itself and it should pop out of the carcass. Use your knife to cut away completely. Remove the wings also if you wish.

2 Mix the fennel and chicory with the carrots in a big bowl and grate in the zest of both the oranges. Pour over the maple syrup, add the fennel seeds and thyme and stir everything together thoroughly to coat.

3 Line a roasting tray with greaseproof paper and scatter over the vegetables. Lay the pieces of guinea fowl on top, drizzle with olive oil and season well with salt and pepper. Cut the oranges in half and put these into the tray as well. They get very juicy as they heat up and will be the dressing for the guinea fowl. Cook in the oven for about 40 minutes until everything is cooked through, and the guinea fowl has nice crispy skin.

4 Remove and allow to rest while you squeeze the oranges over the vegetables and the cooked bird. Carve the crown and serve in pieces and separate the drumstick from the thighs so everyone gets a bit of leg and a bit of breast.

This recipe also works really well with chicken.

A GREAT BIG SALAD OF ROASTED SQUASH, PANEER, RADICCHIO AND PARMA HAM

35

TOTAL

Preparation 10
Cooking 25
Serves 2
or 4 as a side dish

This recipe can also be made using endive if you can't find radicchio.

This really is a great throw-in-the-oven kind of dish that requires only a little preparation in terms of chopping and can be eaten hot, warm or cold. You can have it as your main meal, but I also like it on the side with some roasted fish or maybe a pan-fried pork chop. It's really versatile and full of flavour.

1 butternut squash, skin left on, seeds removed and cut into large chunks
250g paneer, cubed
2 teaspoons runny honey
salt and freshly ground black pepper
1 teaspoon ground cumin
1 teaspoon chilli flakes

2 red radicchio lettuces, cut into eighths
2 tablespoons olive oil, plus extra to drizzle
2 tablespoons balsamic vinegar
12–16 slices Parma or prosciutto ham
juice of 1 lemon
100g rocket

1 Preheat the oven to 200°C/400°F/Gas 6. Line a baking sheet with greaseproof paper and spread out the squash and paneer onto it. Pour over the honey and season with salt, pepper, cumin and the chilli flakes. Scatter the radicchio over the top. Drizzle the whole tray with the olive oil and balsamic vinegar. Cook for about 25 minutes until the radicchio is slightly charred on the thinner parts of the leaves and the honey is caramelising a little on the edges of the paneer.

2 Remove from the oven and transfer to a serving plate. Tear over the ham. Drizzle over the lemon juice, some extra olive oil and scatter on the rocket. Make sure you pour over any juice that might be left in the roasting tray and serve.

STEAMED SEA BREAM WITH GINGER, CHILLI AND SPRING ONION

16

TOTAL

Preparation 10

Cooking 6

Serves 2

as a light dinner

This dish goes really well with the Pineapple Kebabs with Vanilla and Maple Syrup (page 157).

This is a really healthy fish dish packed full of flavour and freshness. It helps to have a bamboo steamer to cook this recipe, but don't worry if you don't have one. An upturned saucer in the bottom of a shallow pan will do the trick as long as your pan has a lid.

2 fillets of sea bream, pin-boned
2 tablespoons light soy sauce
1 teaspoon toasted sesame seed oil
1/2 teaspoon caster sugar
1 tablespoon rice vinegar
3cm piece of fresh ginger, peeled and sliced into very thin strips
1 large green chilli, sliced on the angle
6 spring onions, trimmed and cut into thin strips (as you would see with Peking duck in a Chinese restaurant)

To serve
a large handful of coriander
1 lime, cut into wedges
steamed rice or a selection of green vegetables

1 Put a wok or saucepan with a steamer on the stove (or see the recipe introduction, above) and half fill the wok or saucepan with boiling water. Cover with the lid.

2 Lay the fillets of fish, skin-side down, on a plate that fits inside the steamer. Combine the soy sauce, sesame seed oil, sugar and vinegar in a bowl. Sprinkle the ginger, chilli and half of the spring onions over the fish fillets and pour over all the sauce.

3 Put the plate into the steamer and put the lid on tight. Leave to steam for about 6 minutes until the fish is cooked through.

4 Serve the fish with all the bits on top and tear over the coriander leaves and remaining spring onions. Pour any juices that are on the plate over the fish and serve with a wedge of lime and steamed rice or green vegetables.

SPICED LAMB MEATBALLS WITH PUMPKIN, APRICOT AND TOMATO STEW

55

TOTAL

Preparation 20
Cooking 35
Serves 4–6

This is a Moroccan-ish dish that I cook a lot because you can make copious quantities of it, leave it in the fridge and have it a hundred different ways for the next couple of days, saving you valuable time. I have even been known to make a monster sandwich with the leftover meatballs and sauce.

For the meatballs
500g minced lamb
1 teaspoon ground cumin
1 teaspoon ground coriander
½ teaspoon chilli powder
½ bunch of coriander, finely chopped
4–5 sprigs of mint leaves, finely chopped
1 egg yolk
1 teaspoon salt
freshly ground black pepper
2 tablespoons vegetable oil

For the pumpkin, apricot and tomato stew
2 tablespoons vegetable oil
2 onions, peeled and diced
1 teaspoon ground ginger
2 red chillies, finely chopped

3 garlic cloves, peeled and finely chopped
1 teaspoon ground cumin
1 pumpkin, skin left on, deseeded and diced
100g dried apricots, roughly chopped
2 x 400g tins chopped tomatoes
200ml chicken or vegetable stock

To serve
a small handful of mint leaves, finely chopped
Greek yogurt
Pomegranate and Almond Couscous, see page 43 (optional)

1 To make the meatballs, combine all the ingredients, except for the vegetable oil, really well. Roll into golfball-sized balls and leave on a tray in the fridge while you prepare the stew.

2 Heat 2 tablespoons of oil in a large, heavy bottomed pan and add the onion, ground ginger, chilli and garlic. Soften for 5–6 minutes, then add the ground cumin and cook well. Add the pumpkin, apricots, tinned tomatoes and the stock and bring to the boil, then reduce the heat and allow to simmer for 20 minutes.

3 Meanwhile, heat a large frying pan and 2 tablespoons of vegetable oil. Remove the meatballs from the fridge and fry in the hot oil for about 5 minutes until nicely browned on all sides. Transfer them to the stew using a slotted spoon.

4 Cook for another 5 minutes before serving with a scattering of fresh mint, a dollop of yogurt and the Pomegranate and Almond Couscous, if using.

As well as the suggested couscous, this recipe is also very good stirred through pasta.

BRAISED SAUSAGES WITH GORGONZOLA POLENTA

40

TOTAL

Preparation 10

Cooking 30

Serves 4

This is comfort food at its best. It's basically sausage and mash but without the mashing. Polenta is a really underused ingredient because a lot of people don't really know what to do with it. It's great because it's so simple to prepare and a little goes a long way. Polenta needs to be flavoured as it can be a bit bland and Gorgonzola is perfect as the creamy blue cheese melts easily into the wet polenta. If you are not a blue cheese fan then you can substitute the Gorgonzola for taleggio.

8 good-quality meaty sausages
3 red onions, peeled and sliced or
3 garlic cloves, peeled and chopped or
  1½ teaspoons ready-chopped garlic
a small pinch of chilli flakes
1 teaspoon herbes de Provence
2 teaspoons tomato purée
salt and freshly ground black pepper
150ml red wine
1 tablespoon balsamic vinegar
1 tablespoon liquid beef concentrate
1 teaspoon caster sugar

250ml chicken stock

For the polenta
500ml chicken stock
250ml semi-skimmed milk
1 teaspoon herbes de Provence
250g quick-cook polenta
200g Gorgonzola
50g butter

To serve
freshly grated Parmesan cheese

1 Start by heating a medium-sized frying pan on the stove. Fry the sausages until golden brown on all sides. Remove from the pan and add the onions, garlic, chilli flakes and herbes de Provence. Allow to cook for 5 minutes before adding the tomato purée and stirring well. Season with salt and pepper.

2 Place the sausages back into the pan with the onions, pour in the wine, vinegar, beef concentrate, sugar and chicken stock and simmer for 15–20 minutes until the sausages are cooked through. If the sauce starts to dry out, add a splash of water.

3 Just before you are ready to serve, you can make the polenta. Heat the chicken stock in a saucepan with the milk and herbes de Provence. When the mixture starts to boil, whisk the liquid quickly and slowly pour in the polenta. The mixture should thicken quite quickly. Season with pepper and beat in the Gorgonzola and butter.

4 Serve the polenta immediately divided between four plates, each topped with two sausages and the sauce they were cooked in. Scatter over the freshly grated Parmesan cheese if using.

Don't leave the polenta sitting around for too long or it will start to firm up. It needs to be cooked just before you are ready to serve.

ASIAN NOODLE SOUP WITH PRAWNS

20

TOTAL

Preparation 10

Cooking 10

Serves 2

Add a tin of coconut milk to this soup to give it a Thai feel.

One of the all-time easiest recipes to cook after a long day and, once you've got your cupboard stocked with the right Asian bits, the shopping for this dinner will be nothing more than some fresh herbs and perhaps a few chillies. It's very versatile and can be made with any vegetables, fish or meat that you fancy or happen to have in the fridge.

For the stock
500ml chicken stock
2 garlic cloves, peeled and sliced or
1 teaspoon ready-chopped garlic
1 teaspoon chilli flakes
1 tablespoon sweet chilli sauce
1 tablespoon dark soy sauce
1 tablespoon oyster sauce
½ teaspoon sesame seed oil
salt (optional)

For the soup
200g dried soba noodles or instant noodles
10–12 whole prawns, peeled
2 heads of pak choi, cut into quarters
1 red chilli, sliced
½ bunch of coriander, chopped
3 spring onions, trimmed and cut into slices
1 lime, cut into wedges

1 The key to a good soup is a good stock so the first job is making the broth big and bold in flavour. Pour the stock into a saucepan and place on a high heat. Add the remaining ingredients and allow the broth to come to the boil. Taste it to check for the spicy/salty balance. If necessary, add more sweet chilli sauce or salt to taste.

2 Add the noodles and the prawns and cook for 4–5 minutes until the noodles are cooked through. Fold the pak choi into the soup and cook until the leaves are tender and the stalk still has a crunch, about 2–3 minutes.

3 Serve in deep soup bowls and sprinkle with the sliced chilli, coriander and spring onions. Serve with a wedge of lime on the side.

SHREDDED CHICKEN AND TORTELLINI ONE-BOWL WONDER

15
TOTAL

Preparation 5
Cooking 10
Serves 2

Why not finish off this meal with some Ricotta and Raspberry Fritters (see page 160)?

This dish can be anything you want it to be – a soup, broth or a stew. Call it what you like, all that matters is that it's quick, tasty, healthy and hassle-free.

1 litre chicken stock
150g fresh tortellini with a filling of any flavour
2 big handfuls of broad beans or soya beans (frozen is fine)
150g cooked chicken (pre-bought or left over), shredded

1 courgette, cut into ribbons with a peeler
salt and freshly ground black pepper

To serve
a large handful of basil leaves
Parmesan cheese shavings

1 Pour the chicken stock into a saucepan and bring to the boil. Add the tortellini and broad beans and cook for 3 minutes before adding the shredded chicken and the courgette ribbons. Cook until the chicken is heated through and then season with lots of salt and pepper.

2 Serve in big soup bowls with freshly torn basil and shaved Parmesan cheese.

ORANGE-MARINATED PORK CHOPS WITH A HAZELNUT AND PARSLEY DRESSING

40

TOTAL

Preparation 20
plus, marinating time

Cooking 20

Serves 4

Pork goes perfectly with most things sweet and slightly acidic, so pork and orange is a brilliant combination. This dish has almost no chopping so all that really needs to be done after the dressing is made is to throw the meat on the griddle pan or under a hot grill and wait for it to be cooked.

For the marinade
zest and juice of 2 large oranges
2 tablespoons honey
4 sprigs of thyme, leaves only
1 tablespoon wholegrain mustard
1 tablespoon sherry vinegar
salt and freshly ground black pepper

For the pork chops
4 pork chops on the bone (try to make sure they have a good layer of fat on them)

For the hazelnut and parsley dressing
100g roughly chopped hazelnuts
1 tablespoon wholegrain mustard
zest and juice of 1 orange
2 teaspoons honey
1 teaspoon sherry vinegar
3 tablespoons olive oil
a large bunch of flatleaf parsley, roughly chopped
Radicchio and Parma Ham Salad (see page 16), to serve (optional)

1 To make the marinade combine the orange zest and juice with the honey, thyme, mustard, vinegar and salt and pepper in a large mixing bowl.

2 Score the fat on the pork chops four or five times to stop the chops curling up too much. Place the chops in the marinade and leave to one side while the grill or griddle pan heats up.

3 To make the dressing, toast the hazelnuts by popping them in a heated dry frying pan for 1–2 minutes and then set aside. Mix the mustard with the orange zest and juice, honey, vinegar and olive oil. Season with salt and pepper.

4 The grill or griddle pan should now be hot enough (a griddle pan should be nearly smoking and on the highest heat). Lay the chops under the grill or on the griddle pan and cook for 6–8 minutes until charred in some places (because of the sugar in the marinade) – moving them around should stop this from happening too much. Brush the chops with the marinade during the cooking time to keep them nice and moist. Turn the chops over and cook for a further 6–8 minutes on the other side. Remove from the pan onto a plate and leave to rest.

Fantastic cooked on the barbecue if the sun is shining.

5 To serve, add the hazelnuts and parsley to the dressing mixture. Transfer the chops to individual plates and spoon over the dressing. Serve with the salad on the side.

PAN-ROASTED LAMB WITH CARROT AND FETA SALAD AND REDCURRANT DRESSING

35
TOTAL

Preparation 15
Cooking 20
Serves 4

When I have a salad for my dinner, I want it to be quite substantial and filling, otherwise I'm hungry half an hour later and find myself raiding the biscuit cupboard. I like to have lots of different colours and textures going on and to combine some hot elements with a cold salad.

6 large carrots, peeled and cut into chunky sticks or batons
2 tablespoons runny honey
2 tablespoons olive oil, plus extra for cooking the lamb
2 teaspoons cumin seeds
1 teaspoon ground coriander
salt and freshly ground black pepper
4 lamb neck fillets, weighing about 200g each
200g feta, cubed

3 tablespoons roughly chopped black olives
a small bunch of coriander
150g mixed salad leaves
3 tablespoons pumpkin seeds

For the dressing
2 tablespoons redcurrant jelly
1 tablespoon red wine vinegar
2 tablespoons olive oil
1 teaspoon Dijon mustard

1 Preheat the oven to 200°C/400°F/Gas 6. Mix the carrots in a bowl with the honey, olive oil, cumin seeds, ground coriander and salt and pepper.

2 Line a roasting tray with greaseproof paper and lay out the carrots evenly on the tray. Roast in the oven for about 15–20 minutes or until they are slightly charred around the edges but still have a little bite to them.

3 While the carrots are cooking, heat up a large frying pan on the highest setting. Oil the lamb fillets and season with salt and pepper. Lay them in the smoking hot pan and cook for about 5–6 minutes on each side, depending on the thickness, until the meat is nicely caramelised on the underside and is slightly firm to the touch. Remove the pan from the heat and leave to rest.

4 To make the dressing, combine all the ingredients in a small saucepan and bring to the boil, whisking to remove any lumps. When combined, turn off the heat and set aside.

5 When the carrots are cooked, remove from the oven and place in a large bowl. Scatter in the feta, black olives and salad leaves and season with pepper. Slice the lamb and mix into the salad. Tear in the coriander leaves and mix through before pouring over the redcurrant dressing. Transfer the salad to a large platter and sprinkle over the pumpkin seeds. Eat straight away before the heat wilts the salad leaves.

The dressing can be made in advance and will keep for a week in the fridge.

PEA AND SALMON FISHCAKES

40

TOTAL

Preparation 25
Cooking 15
Serves 4

The main time-consuming element when making fishcakes is the mash, so I wondered if there was an alternative ingredient that I could use to bind the fish together. Peas are perfect for this and also work really well with the flavours of the other ingredients.

For the fishcakes
200g frozen peas (petits pois are best)
200g smoked salmon trimmings
500g salmon, skinned, pin-boned and cut into 1cm pieces
zest of 2 lemons and juice of 1 lemon
a small bunch of dill, roughly chopped
1 egg
3 spring onions, trimmed and chopped
1 tablespoon plain flour
salt and freshly ground black pepper

For the fishcake coating
100g plain flour
2 eggs, beaten
150g fine breadcrumbs or polenta
4 tablespoons olive oil

For the sauce
220ml crème fraîche
zest and juice of 1 lemon
1 tablespoon wholegrain mustard

400g wilted spinach (optional)

1 Put a pan of water to boil with a pinch of salt added on the stove. Once boiling, blanch the peas for 20–30 seconds before draining and running under cold water to cool. Put the peas into a blender along with all the remaining ingredients for the fishcakes, except for the seasoning, and pulse until the mixture has combined. Season with plenty of salt and pepper.

2 Put the flour, eggs and breadcrumbs or polenta into three separate bowls. Make eight patties out of the fishcake mix and pass first though the flour, then the egg and finally the breadcrumbs. Put on a baking tray and leave in the fridge until you are ready to cook them.

3 When you are ready to eat, preheat the oven to 190°C/375°F/Gas 5. Pour the olive oil into a frying pan and turn the heat to medium. Lay the fishcakes in the pan (you will probably need to do this in two or three batches) and cook for about 2–3 minutes until they are golden brown on both sides. Remove the partly cooked fishcakes from the pan, place them back on the baking tray and finish cooking in the oven for 6–8 minutes until cooked through.

4 While they are in the oven, heat up the crème fraîche in a small saucepan together with the lemon zest and juice and the wholegrain mustard. Remove the cooked fishcakes from the oven and serve with the crème fraîche sauce and wilted spinach.

For a quick accompaniment, pierce a bag of spinach a few times and cook in a microwave on high for 3 minutes.

A VERY EASY BAKED RICOTTA PIE

35

TOTAL

Preparation 10

Cooking 25

Serves 4–6

as a dinner with a salad, or 6-8 as an accompaniment

If you fancy something a bit different try adding some fried bacon and caramelised onions to the ricotta before mixing.

I'm not entirely sure where I learnt this recipe, but I do know that I make it all the time, either as a side dish if I have a few people over for dinner, or as a variation of an omelette if I fancy something a bit different. Much like an omelette, you can add whatever ingredients you like, but I also like to eat it on its own with a green salad (making sure there is a little left over in the fridge for the next day, as it's great cold as well).

2 tablespoons olive oil
500g ricotta
2 egg yolks
3 large eggs
220ml crème fraîche

salt and freshly ground black pepper
2 sprigs of thyme, leaves only
75g ready roasted peppers, sliced into thin strips
50g Parmesan cheese, grated

1 Preheat the oven to 200°C/400°F/Gas 6. Grease a medium-sized baking dish with the olive oil. Beat the ricotta and eggs together in a food-processor until light and pale in colour. (This can also be done using an electric whisk.)

2 When pale, add the crème fraîche and mix in well. Season with a large pinch of salt and plenty of pepper. Stir in the thyme leaves, pour the mixture into the baking dish and scatter over the sliced peppers. Poke them down into the mixture so they won't burn. Sprinkle the Parmesan cheese over the top.

3 Bake in the oven for 20–25 minutes. The mixture should be set with a very slight wobble. Leave to cool for 10 minutes before serving.

PANTRY PASTA

20
TOTAL

Preparation 5
Cooking 15
Serves 4

To speed up the cooking time for this recipe (or any pasta recipe), put a little water in the pasta pan and bring it to the boil while also boiling a kettle full of water. Top up the saucepan from the kettle before adding the pasta.

There are some things that we all have in our cupboard and I think it's very important to know how to make them into a tasty dinner. Here, I'm talking pasta; for this dish I like to use penne, but any type will do. Very easy to prepare with everything thrown into one pan so there's hardly any washing up it's ideal if you haven't had time to shop.

salt and freshly ground black pepper
500g dried pasta
2 tablespoons olive oil, plus extra to serve
1 red onion, peeled and chopped
2 garlic cloves, peeled and chopped or
   2 teaspoons ready-chopped garlic
1 x 400g tin chopped tomatoes
125ml white wine
½ teaspoon chilli flakes

1 teaspoon balsamic vinegar
½ teaspoon caster sugar
2 tablespoons capers in vinegar, drained
2 x 200g tins tuna, drained
2 tablespoons pitted black olives

To serve
a small handful of basil leaves (optional)
Parmesan cheese, grated (optional)

1 Put a big pan of water on the stove to boil and add a pinch of salt. When the water starts to boil add the pasta and cook as described on the packet until al dente.

2 Place a frying pan on the stove, add the oil, onion and garlic and allow to soften for 4–5 minutes. Add the tinned tomatoes, white wine, chilli flakes, vinegar and sugar. After a few minutes add the capers, tuna and olives. Season with salt and pepper and allow to simmer while the pasta cooks.

3 Drain the pasta and mix with the sauce. Serve with the basil leaves and grated Parmesan cheese, if you fancy, and a drizzle of olive oil.

ROASTED CHICKEN LEGS WITH PEA, LETTUCE AND PANCETTA STEW

40
___
TOTAL

Preparation 10
Cooking 30
Serves 4

This is the easiest dish to cook with minimal shopping. It can usually be rustled up with things that should be in the freezer such as chicken and petits pois. It's a good idea to keep the freezer stocked with bare essentials and take them out to defrost in the morning. All you then need to do is pick up some baby gem lettuce and double cream on the way home.

4 chicken leg portions
2 tablespoons olive oil
1 teaspoon dried oregano
salt and freshly ground black pepper

For the pea, lettuce and pancetta stew
50g butter
300g smoked lardons or pancetta cubes
2 shallots, peeled and finely sliced
2 garlic cloves, peeled and sliced

1 tablespoon plain flour
4 heads of little gem lettuce, cut into
   quarters
125ml white wine
300ml chicken stock
400g frozen petits pois
a pinch of sugar
100ml double cream
juice of 1 lemon
loaf of crusty bread, to serve

1 Preheat the oven to 190°C/375°F/Gas 5. Start by preparing the chicken legs for roasting. To make sure you get a good crispy skin, rub the legs with the olive oil and season with the oregano and salt and pepper. Put into a roasting tin and cook for about 30 minutes, without turning them over, until the meat is cooked through.

2 When the chicken has been in the oven for 15 minutes start to cook the pea, lettuce and pancetta stew. Put the butter in a deep frying pan or casserole dish and add the lardons or pancetta. Fry until slightly golden for 5–6 minutes before adding the shallots and garlic. Then add the flour and stir well. Season with salt and pepper.

3 Lay the lettuce in the pan, cut-side down, add the wine and stock and bring to the boil. Then reduce the heat and allow the liquid to reduce by half.

4 Add in the peas with the sugar and cream. Bring the mixture up to the boil, stirring gently from time to time to stop anything on the bottom of the pan burning. If your mixture looks a bit dry, add a few tablespoons of water or chicken stock. Add the lemon juice and check for seasoning.

5 Remove the chicken from the oven and serve alongside the stew with crusty bread to mop up the juices.

If you have cream cheese in the fridge it makes a lovely sauce instead of using the double cream.

TRAY-BAKED SALMON WITH PANCETTA, POTATOES, TOMATOES AND ASPARAGUS

40

TOTAL

Preparation 10
Cooking 30
Serves 4

Great with chicken thighs or any meaty fish – I often use monkfish.

This isn't so much a recipe as a mixture of ingredients thrown together that taste great when combined and cook in about the same time. Salmon is a fish that can have a bit of a bad name as people tend to overcook it and serve it with the same old accompaniments. I promise that this combination of flavours and ingredients work in perfect harmony.

4 tablespoons olive oil, plus extra for oiling
8 potatoes
salt and freshly ground black pepper
2 teaspoons dried oregano
4 salmon fillets, weighing about 150–180g each

20 spears of asparagus, trimmed
20 cherry plum tomatoes on the vine, halved
8 slices of pancetta or Parma ham
juice of 1 lemon

1 Preheat the oven to 190°C/375°F/Gas 5. Line a large baking tray with baking parchment and rub with a little oil. Slice the potatoes (with their skins left on) to the thickness of just less than a pound coin. Lay the potatoes over the tray, trying not to overlap them too much. Sprinkle generously with salt and pepper and the oregano and drizzle with 2 tablespoons of olive oil. Put in the hot oven for 15 minutes.

2 Remove the baking tray from the oven and increase the temperature to 220°C/425°F/Gas 7. Lay the salmon fillets on top of the potatoes and scatter around the asparagus spears and tomatoes. Drape the pancetta or Parma ham over the top. Drizzle over the rest of the olive oil and put the tray back in the oven for a further 10–15 minutes until everything is cooked through.

3 Squeeze over the lemon juice and serve immediately.

HONEY-ROASTED PORK FILLET WITH PEARS AND PARSNIPS

50
TOTAL

Preparation 15
Cooking 35
Serves 4–6

Pork combines beautifully with all things sweet and here I'm exploring something a bit different. Pork and pears are a great pairing and parsnips add a nice crispy texture to this dish. Pork fillet can be very tender if cooked correctly as well as being healthy and quick to roast making it the perfect choice for a speedy supper.

2 pork fillets, weighing about 300–400g each
2 tablespoons wholegrain mustard
2 tablespoons runny honey
juice of 2 lemons
2 garlic cloves, peeled and chopped or 2 teaspoons ready-chopped garlic

2 sprigs of thyme, leaves only
4 tablespoons olive oil
2 Comice pears, cored and cut into pieces lengthways
4 parsnips, peeled and cut into pieces lengthways
salt and freshly ground black pepper

1 Preheat the oven to 190°C/375°F/Gas 5. Lay the pork fillets in a wide container. Mix together the mustard, honey, lemon juice, garlic, thyme and olive oil in a jug. Combine well and pour half of the mixture over the pork. Cover and set aside.

2 Mix the pears and parsnips on a roasting tray and pour over the remaining honey and mustard mixture. Try to make sure the parsnips are closer to the edges of the tray as these will take slightly longer to cook. Lay the pork on top and pour over the marinade. Season well with salt and pepper and place in the oven for 35 minutes until the meat is cooked through and the parsnips are tender and slightly crispy.

3 Leave the pork to rest for 5 minutes before carving into slices. Serve with the roasted vegetables and the sauce from the roasting tray.

You can cook the pork in a frying pan to caramelise the outside before transferring to the oven to finish cooking for 15–20 minutes.

TANDOORI-MARINATED MACKEREL WITH RED ONION AND CORIANDER SALAD

25

TOTAL

Preparation 15

Cooking 10

Serves 2

I know there are lots of spices in this recipe, which can be expensive to buy, but once you have them you will use them again and again. Because I'm using this marinade on fish, you don't really have to marinade it at all, which helps speed up the prep time.

For the tandoori marinade
2 teaspoons ground cumin
2 teaspoons ground coriander
2 teaspoons turmeric
½ teaspoon ground cinnamon
2 teaspoons hot paprika
3 garlic cloves, peeled and crushed or
  3 teaspoons ready-chopped garlic
2 red chillies or 2 teaspoons lazy chilli
150ml thick set yogurt
juice of 2 lemons
salt and freshly ground black pepper

For the red onion and coriander salad
3 red onions, left whole, peeled and finely
  sliced into rings
juice of 2 limes
1 teaspoon caster sugar
½ teaspoon salt
a large bunch of coriander, chopped
a handful of mint leaves, chopped
olive oil, for drizzling

For the mackerel
2–3 whole mackerel, gutted
juice of ½ lime

To serve
150ml thick set yogurt
1 lime, cut into wedges

1 Heat the grill to medium. Make the marinade by combining all the ingredients with a large pinch of salt and pepper. Either whizz in a food-processor until smooth or, if using pre-chopped chilli and garlic, simply mix the ingredients together in a bowl. Set aside.

2 To make the salad, combine all the ingredients, except the coriander, mint and oil, and set aside for the flavours to infuse.

3 Take the mackerel and make three deep slashes on the diagonal on both sides of each fish. This will allow the marinade to penetrate the flesh of the fish and also speed up cooking time. Generously cover the fish with the marinade on both sides and lay them on a non-stick grill tray so they are easy to turn over halfway through cooking.

4 Grill the fish for about 5 minutes before turning them over and cooking for a further 5 minutes – the fish is ready when the skin starts to bubble and blister slightly. Put a small knife into the thickest part of one of the incisions and see if the flesh easily comes away. Remove from the grill and squeeze the lime juice over the mackerel.

5 Mix the coriander and mint with the onion salad and drizzle over some olive oil. Serve with the fish accompanied by some yogurt and a wedge of lime.

This marinade works well on most meats and is also fantastic on the barbecue – it can be made up to 3–4 days in advance and stored in the fridge ready to use.

GRILLED GAMMON STEAK, FRIED EGG AND SPICY BEANS

20
TOTAL

Preparation 5
Cooking 15
Serves 2

Breakfast at dinner time?! What else can I say – HEAVEN, and all in 20 minutes. This is my ultimate indulgent naughty feast and it's perfect for a lazy night's supper.

2 teaspoons English mustard
1 teaspoon runny honey
3 tablespoons vegetable oil
salt and freshly ground black pepper
2 chunky gammon steaks, weighing about
    180–200g each
2 large eggs

For the beans
1 x 400g tin black beans
250ml tomato passata
1 teaspoon Worcestershire sauce
½ teaspoon Tabasco sauce
a small bunch of flatleaf parsley, roughly
    chopped

1 Heat a griddle pan or large frying pan on a high heat. Make the marinade by mixing the mustard, honey and 1 tablespoon of oil together. Season with a pinch of salt and pepper and spread over the gammon while your griddle pan or frying pan heats up.

2 Once smoking hot, lay the steaks onto the griddle or frying pan and cook for 4–5 minutes on each side. If it looks like the marinade is charring slightly, move the steaks around in the pan and turn down the heat a little. Brush with any of the remaining marinade. Once the steaks have had their 8–10 minutes cooking, turn off the heat and let them rest while you finish the rest of the meal.

3 This stage can be done while the gammon is cooking. Drain and rinse the beans then add them to a saucepan with the passata and Worcestershire and Tabasco sauces. Simmer for around 10 minutes, stirring from time to time to stop everything from sticking. Season to taste with salt and pepper. Once thickened and hot, sprinkle in the chopped parsley.

4 Finally, heat a frying pan with 2 tablespoons vegetable oil and crack in the eggs. Season the yolks with salt and cook for about 3 minutes until still runny. Serve the fried egg on top of the gammon and the beans on the side.

This makes a great breakfast – with a grilled tortilla and sprinkle of grated cheese you don't even need the gammon!

ROASTED POUSSIN WITH POMEGRANATE AND ALMOND COUSCOUS

45
TOTAL

Preparation 10
plus 5 minutes
resting time
Cooking 35
Serves 4

Poussins are a great dinner time saviour if you don't have time to roast a whole chicken. They cook in half the time and everyone gets their own bird, which means no fights about who gets the breast and who gets the leg! Just like a chicken, you can eat just about anything with them, and I've decided to do a bit of a Moroccan twist with this recipe. You will have a tasty dinner on the table within an hour of walking in the door.

2 lemons, cut in half
4 whole poussins
4 sprigs of thyme
100g butter
salt and freshly ground black pepper

For the couscous
400ml vegetable stock

200g couscous
½ teaspoon chilli flakes
zest and juice of 2 lemons
½ bunch of coriander, chopped
½ bunch of mint, leaves only, chopped
75g toasted flaked almonds
100g pomegranate seeds
50ml olive oil

Pomegranate seeds are available pre-picked from most supermarkets in the prepared fruit section and are a great time-saver to have in your fridge.

1 Preheat the oven to 190°C/375°F/Gas 5. Start by cooking the poussins. Place the lemon halves into the cavity of each bird along with a sprig of thyme in each. Soften the butter between your fingers and rub liberally all over the skin of each poussin. Season with salt and pepper, put into one or two roasting tins and cook in the hot oven for about 35 minutes.

2 While they are cooking, you can prepare the couscous. Heat the stock in a saucepan. Put the couscous in a large bowl and add the chilli flakes and some salt and pepper. Pour the stock over the couscous and cover with clingfilm. Leave for 10–15 minutes for the couscous to steam and swell.

3 Add the lemon zest and juice, chopped herbs, flaked almonds and pomegranate seeds to the couscous. Then drizzle over the olive oil, use a fork to fluff up the couscous and taste for seasoning. Set aside.

4 Once the poussins are cooked, remove from the oven and allow to rest for 5 minutes. Pour any juices from the tray into the couscous before serving alongside the roasted birds.

LAMB CHOPS WITH SMASHED WHITE BEAN CHAMP

20

TOTAL

Preparation 10

Cooking 10

Serves 4

Great to tuck into when you have guests over. Try starting with the Sweetcorn and Spring Onion Fritters (page 137) to whet a few appetites.

This is a dinner that should become part of your weekly menu – it's cheap, uses storecupboard basics, involves hardly any preparation time and tastes great. You can usually get lamb chops for a reasonable price and a tin of butter beans is a very important storecupboard ingredient and therefore should always be available. My style of cooking tends to draw on a few main ingredients – in this case that would be the lamb and the beans – and then I like to jazz things up a bit by adding fresh herbs or a few spices to make a normal evening meal come to life. This dish is no exception.

12 lamb chops or cutlets (with or without the bone)
5 tablespoons extra virgin olive oil
2 tablespoons balsamic vinegar
3 garlic cloves, finely sliced
salt and freshly ground black pepper
75g butter

3 garlic cloves, peeled and grated
2 sprigs of rosemary, leaves only, finely chopped
juice of 1 lemon
2 x 400g tins butter beans, drained
6 spring onions, trimmed and finely sliced

1 Preheat the grill to the highest setting. Place the lamb chops or cutlets in a bowl with 2 tablespoons of the olive oil, all the vinegar, the sliced garlic and a big pinch of salt and pepper. Rub in the marinade well before placing the lamb under the grill and cooking for 5 minutes on each side.

2 While the lamb is cooking, melt the butter in a saucepan and add the garlic and rosemary. When the butter starts to bubble and go slightly nut brown in colour, squeeze in the lemon juice and add the beans and spring onions. Stir well until heated through.

3 Turn off the heat and mash the beans with a potato masher. You don't need a fine paste, lumps are good. Pour in most of the remaining olive oil or enough to get the consistency as you like it. It will be quite firm.

4 Once the lamb chops are cooked, allow them to rest and pour any juices into the bean mash. Taste the mash for seasoning and serve with the lamb.

PRAWN AND EGG FRIED RICE

20
_____
TOTAL

Preparation 10
Cooking 10
Serves 4–6

I absolutely love egg-fried rice, but always avoided making it at home as you have to cook the rice then wait for it to cool. Then I discovered pre-cooked rice, which is perfect for this dish. The chef in me told me that I should always avoid using pre-prepared foods, but here is one that is definitely allowed. You can add whatever you like to this dish; I love big, fat juicy prawns in mine. If you want to bulk it out a bit, you can add other vegetables, such as broccoli, mangetout or green beans, and cooked meats, such as cooked chicken and pork... the list is endless.

400g basmati express rice
3 eggs
2 tablespoons vegetable or groundnut oil
2 red chillies, roughly sliced and seeds left in if you are a fan of spicy food
2 garlic cloves, peeled and roughly chopped or 1½ teaspoons ready-chopped garlic
6 spring onions, trimmed and cut into 2cm pieces with the white and green

parts separated
400g raw large prawns, peeled
4 tablespoons dark soy sauce
1 teaspoon toasted sesame seed oil
2 tablespoons sweet chilli sauce
2 large handfuls of frozen or fresh peas (make sure they are defrosted before using if using frozen peas)
1 lime, cut into wedges
a large bunch of coriander

1 To cook the rice, follow the instructions on the express rice packet (usually put it in the microwave for 2 minutes).

2 Beat the eggs in a bowl. Heat a large wok or frying pan on the stove, add the vegetable or groundnut oil and when the oil is very hot, add the chilli, garlic and white part of the spring onions and stir-fry for 2 minutes. Remove them from the pan and add the beaten eggs, move them around quickly in the pan or wok until cooked and well scrambled – I like to leave some big bits of egg as this is the best part. Remove the scrambled eggs from the pan.

3 Add the cooked ingredients back into the wok or pan along with the prawns, heated rice, soy sauce, sesame seed oil, sweet chilli sauce, green tips of the spring onions and the peas. Stir well and then add the egg back in and heat through for 3–4 minutes. Mix together well and serve with a wedge of lime and torn coriander.

Raw prawns give the best flavour, but if you are in hurry, then cooked prawns are fine for a midweek dinner.

GRIDDLED SWORDFISH STEAK WITH CHERMOULA POTATO SALAD

35

TOTAL

Preparation 10
Cooking 25
Serves 4

Swordfish is a meaty fish that stands up well to strong flavours, making this perfumed chermoula the perfect match. This is a lovely light and healthy dish with bags of flavour. If you make an extra big potato salad, it will be great for lunch the next day, therefore getting two meals out of the way in one cooking session. If you can't get swordfish, tuna or seabass also work very well. Try mixing the chermoula with tinned beans or using it as a marinade. It's great!

1kg new potatoes
4 swordfish steaks, 2cm thick and
**   weighing about 120–150g each**
2 tablespoons olive oil
sea salt and freshly ground black pepper
juice of 1 lemon

2 red chillies, finely chopped
4 garlic cloves, peeled and finely grated
2 teaspoons ground cumin
zest and juice of 2 lemons
6 tablespoons olive oil
1 teaspoon red wine vinegar
100g rocket

For the chermoula
2 large bunches of coriander, finely
**   chopped**

1 Cook the potatoes in boiling salted water until very tender.

2 To make the chermoula, mix the coriander with the chilli and garlic in a large bowl. Add the cumin, lemon zest and juice, olive oil, red wine vinegar and salt and pepper. This can all be done in a blender if you prefer.

3 Once the potatoes are cooked, drain them and return them to the pan they were cooked in. Smash the potatoes with the back of a fork while still hot and pour over two-thirds of the chermoula.

4 Heat a griddle pan until it smokes. Rub the swordfish steaks with a little olive oil and season with sea salt and pepper. Lay onto the hot griddle pan and cook for 5 minutes on each side. Squeeze over the juice of the remaining lemon and turn off the heat.

5 Mix the rocket through the potato and chermoula mixture and divide between serving plates. Lay a swordfish steak on top of each and serve while still warm with the remaining chermoula on the side.

Make a little extra chermoula and it will last a week in the fridge. Put it into a clean Kilner jar and pour a couple of tablespoons of olive oil on top to stop the air getting to it.

GNOCCHI BAKE WITH HOT-SMOKED SALMON AND SPINACH

20

TOTAL

Preparation 5

Cooking 15

Serves 4–6

Try cooking the Baked Apricot Brioche (see page 144) for dessert. Take the gnocchi out of the oven and put the brioche straight in.

Gnocchi is that wonderful dish I order in a restaurant and wish I cooked more at home. The truth is that once you've gone through the process of making gnocchi, so much of the day is lost. Now that's fine if it's raining outside and you have a whole day to spend in the kitchen, but you should know that shop-bought gnocchi is just as good as shop-bought pasta (they are both available in the same section of the supermarket) and we all buy that. This dish has a sharp tang to it and makes a good change to having pasta.

1 x 400g bag young spinach leaves
200g mascarpone cheese
zest and juice of 2 lemons
1 x 75g packet dill, chopped

salt and freshly ground black pepper
300g hot-smoked salmon
500g fresh gnocchi
75g Parmesan cheese, grated

1 Preheat the grill to high and bring a pan of water with a big pinch of salt added to the boil.

2 Make 2–3 holes in the bag of spinach and put it in the microwave at 800W for 2 minutes to wilt. If you don't have a microwave then steam the spinach until slightly wilted.

3 Put the mascarpone cheese into a saucepan and add the lemon zest and juice and dill, and season with salt and pepper. Stir over a low heat until the mascarpone has melted, then add the wilted spinach and flake in the salmon. Try to keep the salmon pieces quite big.

4 Put the gnocchi into the saucepan of boiling water and cook for 3 minutes. Drain and return to the saucepan and then stir in the salmon sauce. Pour the whole lot into a baking dish and cover with the grated Parmesan. Grill for 3–5 minutes until the top bubbles and is golden brown.

SPICY BEEF SAUSAGE AND RICOTTA NAAN PIZZAS

25

TOTAL

Preparation 10
Cooking 15
Serves 4

Try with My Chop Salad on the side (see page 129).

We all love pizza – it's loaded with everything we like and, best of all, it's one of the few dinners we are allowed to eat with our fingers. But pizza dough is really something that needs time and, let's face it, time is something that a lot of us don't often have. So this is my own quick version and I love it! If you can't find the spicy beef sausages, you can spice it up with sliced pepperoni or by adding some chopped chillies.

2 tablespoons tomato purée
4 naan breads (plain or flavoured)
200g ricotta cheese
4 uncooked spicy beef sausages
2 red onions, left whole, peeled and finely sliced into rings

4 pinches of chilli flakes
4 pinches of ground cumin
salt and freshly ground black pepper
2 tablespoons olive oil, plus extra for drizzling
100g rocket

1 Preheat the oven to 220°C/425°F/Gas 7. Mix the tomato purée with 2 tablespoons of water to loosen it and spread a small amount over each naan bread. Leave a border around the edge as you would with a pizza.

2 Crumble the ricotta cheese onto each naan. Remove the sausages from their skins and evenly distribute the meat between all four. Scatter on the onion slices and add a pinch of chilli flakes and ground cumin to each one. Season with salt and lots of pepper. Drizzle with the olive oil and place into a hot oven for 15 minutes.

3 Remove the naans from the oven, scatter with the rocket and drizzle with a little more olive oil. Serve immediately.

Watching
the Pennies

When times are tough and money is a little tight, going out to eat is an expense that few people can afford. I want to give a few tips on how to make a great dinner without having to spend a fortune and, of course, in quick time. This chapter should appeal to all your family and friends. If you're really smart about what you cook, where you buy your food and use seasonal ingredients when possible, you can make some fantastic tasty food while still on a budget. If you're cooking for friends, make sure they bring the wine!

CHICKEN AND BUTTER BEAN CASSOULET

60
TOTAL

Preparation 5
Cooking 55
Serves 4

Chicken thighs are extremely reasonable to buy and have a much better flavour than the breast. They don't dry out while cooking and lend themselves very well to slow-cooked dishes. The great thing about this dinner is that once the minimal chopping and browning is done there is very little left for you to do, allowing you the luxury of time to relax while your dinner cooks.

2 tablespoons vegetable oil
4 chicken thighs
4 chicken drumsticks
salt and freshly ground black pepper
200g smoked lardons or smoked bacon
    rashers, chopped
1 large red onion, peeled and finely diced
3 garlic cloves, peeled and sliced
1 bay leaf
1 teaspoon dried oregano

1 tablespoon tomato purée
2 x 400g tins butter beans, drained
    and rinsed
125ml white wine
2 x 400g tins plum tomatoes
1 teaspoon caster sugar
100g dried breadcrumbs
75g Parmesan cheese, grated

1 Preheat the oven to 200°C/400°F/Gas 6. Heat a large, deep frying pan or an ovenproof casserole dish on a high heat with the vegetable oil. Season the chicken with salt and pepper and gently fry in the pan or casserole dish until all sides are golden brown, about 5 minutes in total.

2 Remove the chicken from the pan, wipe out any slightly burnt bits with kitchen paper and add the lardons or bacon. Increase the heat and allow the bacon to crisp a little. Add the onion with the garlic and allow to soften. Then add the bay leaf and oregano, followed by the tomato purée and mix well. Finally add the butter beans and give it one more stir.

A great alternative is to substitute the chicken with monkfish or some large peeled king prawns.

3 Return the chicken to the pan, mix around well and pour in the white wine and the plum tomatoes. The stew now needs to simmer slowly for 25 minutes. Season with the sugar and salt and pepper.

4 Once the mixture starts to thicken, reduce the heat and sprinkle over the breadcrumbs and Parmesan cheese. Put in the hot oven, uncovered, for 15–20 minutes until the breadcrumbs are nice and crispy. Serve.

PAN ROASTED BEETROOT, SOFT GOAT'S CHEESE, MINT AND BROAD BEAN SALAD

20

TOTAL

Preparation 10

Cooking 10

Serves 2

as a light dinner
or 4 as a side dish

This is a colourful and lively dish that will please most people. It is lovely as a healthy dinner on its own and is so quick and easy it can also be made as a side dish to accompany your main meal. Buy good-quality young goat's cheese to ensure a nice fresh flavour and if you can't get hold of broad beans, soya beans are also very good. Beetroot is often overlooked as a vegetable and I think that this simple dish really does it justice.

1 tablespoon olive oil
8 small ready-cooked beetroots, cut into
   quarters
2 tablespoons balsamic vinegar
3 sprigs of fresh thymes, leaves only
a pinch of sugar
100g broad beans or soya beans (fresh if in
   season or frozen)
a bunch of mint, leaves only, finely
   shredded

75g toasted hazelnuts, lightly crushed
200g soft goat's cheese
a small handful of basil leaves

For the dressing
1 tablespoon Dijon mustard
zest and juice of 1 lemon
1 tablespoon runny honey
2 tablespoons olive oil
salt and freshly ground black pepper

1 Preheat a frying pan with the olive oil. Put the beetroot into the pan and season with salt. Cook on a high heat for 6 minutes until the beetroot is charred on the edges, then add the balsamic vinegar, the thyme leaves and a pinch of sugar. Turn down the heat and allow the beetroot to colour some more for a further 3–5 minutes.

2 Remove the beets from the pan, reduce the heat to the lowest setting and add the ingredients for the dressing to the pan juices. Mix well and season with salt and pepper. Remove from the heat.

3 If the broad beans are frozen, put them in a heatproof bowl, pour a kettle of boiling water over them to defrost them and drain. Put the beans back into the bowl and lightly crush with the back of a fork, keeping some whole. Then add the shredded mint leaves and hazelnuts and pour over half of the dressing from the frying pan.

4 Scatter the warm caramelised beets over a big platter, crumble over the soft goat's cheese and scatter over the crushed broad beans and mint mixture. Pour over the remaining warm dressing and decorate with the basil leaves. Serve.

For a quicker alternative to chopping the hazelnuts you can wrap them in clingfilm and crush using a rolling pin or the base of a saucepan.

MINUTE STEAK SANDWICH WITH FRIED ONIONS AND SWEET MUSTARD

20

TOTAL

Preparation 5

Cooking 15

Serves 1

as a light dinner or
2 as a side dish

Accompany
with the
Chunky Potato
Wedges (see
page 123) and
finish with An
Easy Mess (see
page 151).

A very thin frying steak is the cheapest quick-cook steak you'll find and it is most definitely the best for a big hearty sandwich. This is such a naughty dinner, but it's perfect for a night in on your own.

2 tablespoons vegetable oil
2 large onions, peeled and sliced
2 very thin frying steaks, weighing 100g each
salt and freshly ground black pepper

1 ciabatta or baguette or preferred bread, toasted
20g butter, softened
2 tablespoons sweet American mustard

1 Place a frying pan on the stove and add half the oil along with the onions. Fry on a high heat for 10 minutes until golden brown and a little crispy around the edges.

2 Move the cooked onions over to the edge of the pan and increase the heat. Add another tablespoon of oil. Season the steaks on both sides with salt and pepper and put them in the pan. Cook for 45 seconds on each side. Turn off the heat and take the steaks out of the pan to rest.

3 Cut your chosen bread in half and toast on both sides either on the griddle or under the grill. Spread with butter and loads of mustard. Pile on the onions and slice the steak before loading onto the sandwich. Put on the top half of toasted bread and dunk into more mustard while you eat.

CORNED BEEF HASH FRITTATA

Eggs are a great base for a variety of ingredients and you can add just about anything to a frittata – try chorizo, smoked paprika and roasted peppers as well.

45
TOTAL

Preparation 10

Cooking 35

Serves 2
as a light dinner
or 4–6 as a side dish

King Edward potatoes are good for this dish as they hold together well when cooked.

2 large potatoes, peeled and cut into
  1cm cubes
salt and freshly ground black pepper
1 tablespoon vegetable oil
2 large onions, peeled and sliced

2 x 200g tins corned beef, cut into
  1cm cubes
2 tablespoons Worcestershire sauce
4 eggs
tomato ketchup (optional), to serve

1 Preheat the oven to 180°C/350°F/Gas 4. Put the potatoes in a saucepan, add boiling water from the kettle, a big pinch of salt and cook for about 8 minutes until tender.

2 Meanwhile, heat the biggest ovenproof non-stick frying pan you have and add the vegetable oil. Add the onions to the pan and cook for 6–7 minutes until soft (it's okay if they colour a bit).

3 Drain the potatoes and add these to the onions. Cook for a further 5 minutes before adding the corned beef. Heat through and mix together with the Worcestershire sauce and lots of salt and pepper.

4 Beat the eggs in a bowl, increase the heat under the corned beef and potatoes and pour in the egg mixture. Stir around in the pan for about 5 minutes until the egg starts to set. Transfer the pan to the oven for about 15 minutes until the egg is almost completely set. Serve with a big blob of ketchup if you wish.

PENNE AND SAUSAGE RAGÙ

50

TOTAL

Preparation 10
Cooking 40
Serves 4

Here is a fantastic quick-time ragù recipe that makes a great change to the old staple spaghetti Bolognese. It is lovely to make and keep a stash of in the freezer, ready to defrost in serious pasta emergencies. I cook this regularly, always with a slight difference, but the basics always stay the same – onions, garlic, tinned tomatoes and the good old humble sausage (I like to use a spicy herb variety).

1 tablespoon olive oil
1 large red onion, peeled and finely
    chopped
½ teaspoon chilli flakes
3 garlic cloves, peeled and finely chopped
salt and freshly ground black pepper
1 bay leaf
4 good-quality sausages of your choosing

1 tablespoon tomato purée
125ml red wine
1 x 400g tin chopped tomatoes
1 teaspoon balsamic vinegar
½ teaspoon caster sugar
2 tablespoons mascarpone
500g dried penne
50g Parmesan cheese, to serve

1 Place a large frying pan or casserole dish on a medium heat and pour in the olive oil. Add the onion, chilli and garlic followed by a pinch of salt. Tear the bay leaf slightly and add to the onion mix and allow everything to sweat and cook gently for 5–6 minutes.

2 Meanwhile, remove the sausages from their skins and break up the meat. Increase the heat under the onions and add the sausagemeat. Stir around in the onions until the meat starts to colour and then add the tomato purée and mix well. Try to break up the sausagemeat as much as you can in the pan and stop it clumping into meaty lumps.

3 Pour in the wine, tomatoes and vinegar and stir in the sugar and mascarpone. Season again and let the mixture boil and bubble for about 15 minutes. Stir occasionally to prevent the ragù sticking to the base of the pan. Reduce the heat and allow the mixture to simmer away gently while you cook the pasta.

4 Put a big pan of water on the stove to boil and add a pinch of salt. When the water starts to boil, add the pasta and cook as described on the packet. Drain the pasta, return it to the pan and add the sausage ragù.

5 Divide between four plates and serve with Parmesan shavings over the top.

For a change, try adding mozzarella and fresh basil to the ragù just before serving.

TURKEY ESCALOPES WITH SAGE BUTTER

25

TOTAL

Preparation 10
Cooking 15
Serves 2

This recipe is particularly simple to prepare, requiring little peeling or chopping. Turkey escalopes are far cheaper to buy than chicken breasts (they are sometimes called turkey steaks) and taste just as good, making them a great alternative.

2 turkey escalopes
4 tablespoons plain flour
1 large egg
8 tablespoons dried breadcrumbs
salt and freshly ground black pepper

6 tablespoons vegetable oil
75g butter
8–10 sage leaves
juice of 1 lemon

1 The turkey escalopes need to be as thin as possible. So if they're looking a bit chunky, put them into a sandwich bag, lay flat and give them a good bashing with a rolling pin until they are about 2mm thick all over.

2 Put the flour, egg and breadcrumbs into separate bowls. Season the flour well, then place the escalopes first into the seasoned flour, then coat well in the egg and finally in the breadcrumbs.

3 Heat a large frying pan on a high heat and pour in all the oil. When the oil is hot, lay in the breaded turkey escalopes and cook for 4–5 minutes on each side until they are golden brown.

4 Remove them from the pan with a slotted spoon or fish slice and lay onto kitchen paper. Pour the oil from the pan into a glass jar or container and wait for it to cool down before throwing it away. Place the frying pan back on the stove on a medium heat and add the butter. When the butter starts to foam, add the sage leaves and lemon juice and cook for a further 20–30 seconds.

5 To serve, put the escalopes onto individual plates and pour over the foaming butter. Add spoonfuls of the Gorgonzola Polenta alongside, if using.

Try serving with the Gorgonzola Polenta (see page 23).

COURGETTE, BASIL AND CHILLI LINGUINE WITH CRÈME FRAÎCHE

A healthy and tasty meal that can be prepared in minutes. You don't need to resort to takeaway or pre-made dinners – this dish can be on the table within 20 minutes of walking through the door.

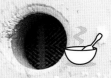

20
___
TOTAL

Preparation 5
Cooking 15
Serves 4

Try using cooked ham and a few fresh peas when in season.

500g dried linguine
2 tablespoons olive oil, plus extra to drizzle
½ teaspoon chilli flakes
2 garlic cloves, peeled and chopped
4 large courgettes, roughly grated

juice of 1 lemon
15 basil leaves
4–5 tablespoons crème fraîche
salt and freshly ground black pepper
100g Parmesan cheese, grated

1 Put a big pan of water on the stove to boil and add a pinch of salt. When the water starts to boil, add the pasta and cook as described on the packet until al dente.

2 Heat the olive oil in a small pan on a very low heat with the chilli flakes and garlic. Turn off the heat once they start to cook and bubble.

3 Drain the pasta and add back into the pan it was cooked in. Stir in the chilli, garlic and warmed olive oil. Then add the courgettes, lemon juice and basil and stir through the crème fraîche. Season well with salt and pepper.

4 Serve with a drizzle of olive oil and the grated Parmesan cheese.

A BIG BOWL OF CURRIED MUSSELS

25
TOTAL

Preparation 10
Cooking 15
Serves 4

These are great
with Chunky
Potato Wedges
(see page 123).

Mussels are a fabulous cheap product and tend to be very widely available. They are instant food and very good for you, too. Few foods give you your very own pair of tongs to use while eating as well, so there's no need for cutlery, just use an empty shell.

2.5kg uncooked mussels, cleaned
1 tablespoon vegetable oil
2 shallots, peeled and sliced
¼ teaspoon chilli powder
½ teaspoon ground cumin

1 tablespoon medium curry powder
200ml coconut milk
2 limes, 1 freshly squeezed for its juice and the other cut into wedges
½ bunch of coriander

1 Tip all the mussels into a sink of cold water. Sort through them, throwing away any that may be broken or open. To check if the mussel is alive, tap its shell on the surface: if the open mussel closes, it's alive and fine to eat; if it doesn't close, throw it away. While you are doing this, pull off any beards that may be on the mussels.

2 Put a large pan with a tight-fitting lid on the stove and add the vegetable oil. Put in the shallots and sweat until translucent. Sprinkle in all the spices and mix well in the pan. Cook for 5 minutes to allow the flavour of the spices to develop.

3 Add all the mussels and the coconut milk to the pan and turn the heat up to high. Put on the lid and cook the mussels for 5–6 minutes, shaking the pan regularly, until heated through and the mussels have all opened up (discard any that won't open).

4 Transfer the mussels to four large bowls together with the cooking liquid. Squeeze over the juice of 1 lime and tear in the fresh coriander leaves. Serve with another wedge of lime on the side if you wish.

LAMB'S LIVER WITH BACON AND SWEET POTATO MASH

35

TOTAL

Preparation 15
Cooking 20
Serves 4

Liver is a fantastic ingredient – inexpensive and very quick to cook. I've suggested lamb's liver, but if you are feeling flush, try calf's liver instead. However, the best part about this dish is the cheat's way of cooking the sweet potato mash, no peeling or boiling water needed here. Just a little gentle scooping and you're away. Have a go... you'll never make normal mash again.

4 sweet potatoes
4 smoked bacon rashers, finely chopped
2 tablespoons olive oil
2 shallots, peeled and finely chopped
100g butter

salt and freshly ground black pepper
2 tablespoons soured cream
4 thick slices of lamb's liver, weighing about 100–120g each
3 tablespoons balsamic vinegar

1 Take the sweet potatoes and make three or four small stab marks all over them. Put into the microwave and cook at 800W for 15 minutes.

2 While they are cooking, heat a frying pan and add the bacon. Turn the heat to medium and allow it to crisp and caramelise. After 5–6 minutes, add 1 tablespoon of the olive oil and the shallots and cook with the bacon for about 5 minutes until the shallots are soft and translucent. This will make them super sweet. Turn off the heat if they are ready before the sweet potatoes.

3 When you hear the ping of the microwave, check to see if the potatoes are very tender and squashy inside. If not, give them a few more minutes. Once cooked, remove the potatoes and cut them in half. Using a spoon, scoop out the filling into a bowl.

Cook large baking potatoes in the microwave and when really soft scoop out the insides, add butter, soured cream and some chopped spring onions for quick, hassle-free champ.

4 Turn on the heat under the bacon and shallots again and add two-thirds of the butter. When it has melted, tip the bacon and shallot mixture into the bowl with the sweet potato filling and mash using a fork or a potato masher. Season well with lots of pepper but go easy on the salt as the bacon is already salty. Finally, add the soured cream, mix well and set aside while you cook the liver.

5 Place the frying pan back on the highest heat and pour in the remaining olive oil. Season the liver with salt and pepper and put it in the hot pan. Cook for 2 minutes on each side. During the final minute of cooking, add the remaining butter and the vinegar.

6 Serve the liver with the sweet potato mash and drizzle over the pan juices.

TASTY LAMB STEW

50–60
TOTAL

Preparation 10
Cooking 40–50
Serves 6–8

A really tasty alternative to the lamb stock is a couple of tins of beef consommé.

Effectively an Irish stew but I didn't want to offend anyone by changing the recipe slightly to be as simple as possible using the good old bare bones of this classic, tasty stew. It is a stew to warm you from the inside out. It's comfort food for me and sometimes only comfort will do.

2.5 litres lamb stock
450g lamb neck fillet, cut into 3cm chunks
400g potatoes, peeled and roughly cut into 3cm chunks
2 bay leaves
3 carrots, peeled and cut into sticks
2 leeks, trimmed, white part roughly chopped
2 large onions, peeled and roughly chopped
2 celery sticks, trimmed and roughly chopped
salt and freshly ground black pepper
a small handful parsley, chopped

1 Put the stock in a large saucepan on a medium heat and add the lamb. Bring to the boil and skim off any impurities before adding the potatoes and bay leaves. Reduce the heat and leave the stew to simmer for 10 minutes.

2 Add all the remaining vegetables, season with salt and pepper and leave to simmer for a further 30–40 minutes until everything is cooked through. Before serving, sprinkle the parsley on top.

TUNA, RED ONION AND BEAN SALAD WITH A SOFT-BOILED EGG

15

TOTAL

Preparation 10
Cooking 5
Serves 2

Why not make this a more substantial meal by serving with An Easy Tart (see page 133)? You can take any leftovers to work for lunch the next day.

A super-simple throw together meal that costs just pennies, this is a perfect weeknight dinner. We should all have these ingredients in our cupboard or lurking in the bottom of the fridge so it requires little shopping making it a brilliant standby recipe.

2 large eggs
300g green beans, trimmed
1 x 200g tin of tuna in water, drained
1 x 225g tin borlotti beans, drained
1 red onion, peeled and finely sliced
1 bag mixed salad leaves

salt and freshly ground black pepper

For the dressing
1 tablespoon red wine vinegar
1 tablespoon Dijon mustard
2 tablespoons olive oil

1 Bring a small saucepan of water to the boil. Carefully put the eggs into the water, reduce the temperature and simmer for exactly 4 minutes 30 seconds. Add the green beans for the last minute of cooking. Remove the pan from the stove, drain into a colander and run cold water over to cool.

2 Mix the tuna and the borlotti beans in a serving bowl and then add the green beans and the red onion.

3 Make the dressing by combining all the ingredients in a small bowl and pour three-quarters over the tuna mixture.

4 Carefully peel the eggs – they will be very soft so watch you don't break them.

5 Mix the salad leaves through the tuna salad and dress with the rest of the dressing. To finish, cut open the eggs and place two halves on each plate, seasoning with a pinch of salt and pepper.

CARAMELISED CHICKEN

25

TOTAL

Preparation 5
Cooking 20
Serves 2

This homely dish has to be followed by the Banana Pudding with Toffee Sauce (see page 155).

This is the perfect midweek supper. It's tasty, cheap and quick to prepare. Everyone will love it and once you've made it once you can become as experimental with it as you like. This is a recipe that will be in your repertoire for years to come.

For the marinade
1 teaspoon dried thyme
2 tablespoons dark soft brown sugar
3 tablespoons Worcestershire sauce
½ teaspoon chilli flakes or chilli paste
2 tablespoons balsamic vinegar
2 tablespoons dark soy sauce
2 tablespoons tomato ketchup

3 tablespoons olive oil

For the chicken
4 chicken legs
4 large red onions, peeled and cut into wedges
10 cherry tomatoes on the vine
4 large baking potatoes, to serve

1 Preheat the oven to 200°C /400°F/Gas 6. Put all the marinade ingredients in a big sandwich bag, add the chicken and the onion wedges. Shake around so all the ingredients get well coated in the marinade.

2 When you are ready to cook, put the chicken legs into a roasting dish with the marinade, onions and the tomatoes. Cook in the oven for 15–20 minutes until the chicken is cooked through. The tomatoes should burst and the onions will go crispy around the edges. Meanwhile, cook the potatoes in the microwave at 800W for 8 minutes – you can pop them in the oven with the chicken when they are done to crisp up the skins.

3 To serve, put the potatoes on plates and add the chicken, roast tomatoes and onion together with the marinade.

BASIL, PINE NUT AND PARMESAN RISOTTO

30
TOTAL

Preparation 10
Cooking 20
Serves 4

This effectively is a pesto risotto, which is one of my favourites. I always think a risotto should be packed with relatively simple, yet strong flavoured, ingredients to make it interesting and exciting, but not overly complex. For this recipe, the pesto is made by just throwing all the ingredients in without blitzing them. Nice and easy!

1.5 litres vegetable or chicken stock
2 tablespoons olive oil
1 leek, trimmed and white part finely
  chopped
2 garlic cloves, peeled and finely chopped
salt
350g risotto rice
50g butter

200ml white wine
100g toasted pine nuts
1 tablespoon mascarpone cheese
a large handful of basil leaves
100g Parmesan cheese, grated, plus a little
  extra for shaving
zest of 2 lemons

1 Heat up the stock on the stove and leave to one side with a ladle in the pan ready to feed the risotto in a few minutes time.

2 Place a large, deep-sided casserole or frying pan on the stove and heat to a low temperature. Add the olive oil to the pan along with the leek and garlic. Add a pinch of salt and cook for a 3–5 minutes until soft. Pour in the rice, add the butter and stir well to coat all the rice grains in the butter and oil.

3 Increase the heat under the pan and add the white wine. Stir the rice until all the wine has been absorbed. Then add a ladleful of stock. You must stir at all times. Keep adding the stock a little at a time until the rice is cooked but still has a slight bite to it.

4 When you are happy with the texture of your risotto, add the pine nuts, mascarpone, torn basil leaves, Parmesan cheese and lemon zest. Stir in well and serve with a few extra shavings of the cheese.

If really pushed for time you can use shop-bought pesto but try to buy it from the deli or refrigerated section to ensure a fresh flavour and vibrant colour.

SMOKED MACKEREL, NEW POTATO AND HORSERADISH SALAD

Smoked mackerel keeps for ages in the fridge so it's not only cheap, it's also got a long shelf life, something of a bonus if you don't get to go to the supermarket as often as you might like. Horseradish is an essential in everyone's fridge and, well, we all need potatoes. Serve this dish with a green salad.

20
TOTAL

Preparation 5
Cooking 15
Serves 4

Crème fraîche is available in both full-fat and half-fat versions. The half-fat is just as tasty and fine to use in this recipe if you wish.

15–20 new potatoes, halved if quite large
4 smoked mackerel fillets
1 x 75g packet chives, snipped
2 tablespoons hot horseradish sauce
2 tablespoons crème fraîche
juice of 1 lemon
2 teaspoons mustard seeds
salt and freshly ground black pepper

1 Place a pan of water on the stove and bring to the boil. Add a pinch of salt and the potatoes. Bring back up to the boil, then reduce the heat and leave to simmer for 10–12 minutes until tender, drain and return to the pan.

2 While the potatoes are still warm, flake in the mackerel fillets along with the chives, horseradish and crème fraîche. Add the lemon juice, mustard seeds and salt and pepper.

CHUNKY HAM, WHITE BEAN AND LEEK CASSEROLE

25

TOTAL

Preparation 10
Cooking 15
Serves 4

This recipe contains my favourite discovery yet – go to the deli counter at your supermarket and ask for ham ends. Sometimes they have them on display and sometimes not, but they are the odd nobbly bits that can't be used to make the perfect slice of ham when they carve the meat off the bone, so they never get used. They are brilliant and such a cheap way to bulk out an evening meal. Throw them into soups, pies or this casserole.

50g butter
3 whole leeks, trimmed and white parts cut into thin slices
2 x 400g tins cannellini beans (although any other white beans will do), drained
400g ham ends (or gammon), cut into chunks

500ml vegetable stock
2 tablespoons cream cheese
2 tablespoons wholegrain mustard
salt and freshly ground black pepper
1 lemon
crusty bread, to serve (optional)

1 Put a casserole dish or saucepan onto the stove on a medium heat. Add the butter and then the leeks and cook them for about 10 minutes until they have wilted and softened. Keep stirring so they don't burn.

2 Add the beans and the ham ends along with the vegetable stock, cream cheese and the mustard. Season with lots of black pepper but take it easy on the salt as the ham will be quite salty; indeed, you might well find that you don't need any at all. Bring the sauce to the boil before adding a squeeze of lemon juice. (If you are using gammon steaks you will need to allow the stew to simmer for 30 minutes before adding the lemon juice to allow the meat to become tender.)

3 Serve in bowls alongside slices of crusty bread, if you wish.

This dish is just as good, if not better, the next day for a really warming lunch.

SMOKED HADDOCK PILAF

50
TOTAL

Preparation 15
Cooking 35
Serves 4

Technically, this dish is called kedgeree and is eaten at breakfast time, but I've never really understood that. Rice and spices first thing in the morning doesn't necessarily appeal to everyone so I've changed the name and have made a few simple changes to this classic dish to speed up the process. This is easy cooking, just a little chopping, add a few different spices and throw everything in the oven. It's also very cheap to prepare and a little goes a long way.

750ml chicken stock
2 large or 3 small undyed smoked
  haddock fillets
2 tablespoons vegetable oil
50g butter
3 large onions, peeled and sliced
salt and freshly ground black pepper

1 teaspoon turmeric
2 teaspoons medium curry powder
400g basmati rice
4 teaspoons sultanas
a small bunch of coriander, chopped or torn
4 soft-boiled eggs, peeled and halved
  (optional)

1 Preheat the oven to 180°C/350°F/Gas 4. Pour the stock into a large saucepan and add the smoked haddock. Turn on the heat and bring the stock to the boil. As soon as it starts to boil, remove the pan from the heat and leave to cool.

2 Place a shallow casserole dish on a medium heat and add the oil and butter. Cook the onions for 4–5 minutes until they have softened. Season well with 1 teaspoon of salt and plenty of black pepper.

3 Add the turmeric and the curry powder followed by the rice and the sultanas. Stir well to coat the rice with the spices.

4 Remove the haddock from the pan and place it on a plate to one side. Pour the cooking liquor into the casserole.

This dish can be cooked on a low heat with a lid on top if you don't have enough time (or patience) to wait for the oven to preheat.

5 Put on a lid, if you have one, or improvise with tin foil and transfer to the oven. Cook for 20–25 minutes until all the liquid has been absorbed and the rice is tender. Check after 10 minutes as you may need to add a little more stock if the rice is looking dry and still not cooked. When the rice is 5 minutes from being cooked – tender but still with a little bite to it – then flake in the smoked fish, being careful to avoid bones and skin. Stir into the rice and cook for a further 5 minutes.

6 Sprinkle with the chopped or torn coriander before you serve. Place the eggs on top, if using.

MINESTRONE STEW

35

TOTAL

Preparation 15
Cooking 20
Serves 4

This is a brilliant dinner that all the family can enjoy. Even though it's classically called a soup, this recipe is definitely substantial enough to be eaten as your main meal because it's more of a thick stew. The pasta makes it a wholesome dinner and the vegetables provide a good chunk of your five-a-day.

2 tablespoons olive oil
250g smoked lardons or smoked bacon
   rashers, chopped
2 carrots, peeled and chopped into 1cm
   dice
2 celery sticks, trimmed and chopped
   into 1cm dice
2 courgettes, chopped into 1cm dice
1 large onion, peeled and chopped into
   1cm dice
1 garlic clove, peeled and chopped or
   1 teaspoon ready-chopped garlic
4 large ripe tomatoes, quartered
1 bay leaf

a pinch of chilli flakes
2 sprigs of thyme, leaves only
2 tablespoons tomatoes purée
1.5 litres chicken or vegetable stock
   (made from a stock cube or bought
   stock)
salt and freshly ground black pepper
200g conchigliette (tiny baby shell pasta)
4 outer leaves of Savoy cabbage, shredded

To serve
crusty bread (optional)
Parmesan cheese shavings (optional)

1 Pour the olive oil in the base of a large saucepan over a medium heat. Add the lardons or chopped bacon and cook for 3–4 minutes until slightly golden brown. Then add the vegetables, garlic and tomatoes, but not the cabbage. Also add the bay leaf, chilli flakes, thyme and tomato purée. Stir everything around well in the pan until all the vegetables are coated in the purée.

2 Add the stock, increase the heat and bring the soup to the boil. Then add salt and pepper followed by the pasta. Allow to boil for about 10 minutes until the pasta is tender. You may need to add a little more stock or water just to cover the pasta completely. Once the pasta is cooked, add the cabbage and allow it to wilt for 2–3 minutes.

3 Serve the soup either with crusty bread or just as it is – I personally like to add a little shaved Parmesan cheese and another twist of black pepper.

Make in big batches and freeze leftovers for a great instant dinner.

CREAMY MACARONI CHEESE

30
TOTAL

Preparation 5
Cooking 25
Serves 4

To make your own breadcrumbs, cut an old loaf of bread into 2–3cm chunks. Place on a baking tray, drizzle with olive oil and bake in an oven at 190°C/375°F/Gas 5 for 5–6 minutes. Remove from the oven and blitz in a blender until smooth.

Macaroni cheese has to be one of the top ten comfort foods. The problem with the traditional macaroni cheese recipe is that it involves making a cheese sauce, which is fine if you have the time, but I know many people who often don't. This recipe is a bit of a cheat, but that's what we like. It is also really good made with ham, cooked chicken or even mushrooms.

500g fresh macaroni or penne
100g Boursin
3 tablespoons cream cheese
250g mozzarella cheese

a large handful of basil leaves
4 handfuls of breadcrumbs
50g Parmesan cheese, grated

1 Preheat the grill to medium. Bring a pan of water to the boil, add a pinch of salt and add the pasta. Cook for 3–4 minutes, if fresh, and according to the packet instructions if dried until al dente.

2 Put the Boursin and cream cheese in a small saucepan. Heat it and mix well until the Boursin has melted into a sauce. Drain the pasta, leaving a little of the water in the bottom of the pan. Put the pasta back into the pan and add the melted Boursin and cream cheese. Tear in the mozzarella, add the basil leaves and pour into a baking dish. Sprinkle over the breadcrumbs and the Parmesan cheese and grill until golden brown. Serve immediately.

Posh Nosh

Just because you may have had a busy day, doesn't mean you shouldn't be able to cook a few close friends or someone special a lovely dinner. In this chapter I'm going to show you that you can have an elegant dinner that takes no time at all to create. If you are entertaining, you want to be in the kitchen for as little time as possible so you have more time to spend with your guests. My key advice when preparing a slightly 'posher' dinner is try to get a step ahead of the game. This might mean laying the table the night before, so when you come home and start cooking that little detail that can often throw us is already done. Also, make sure you know the recipe – just have a quick read through before you start cooking. This way you will be a bit more familiar with it and cooking will be a far more enjoyable experience.

ROASTED HALIBUT WITH LENTIL AND SUNBLUSH TOMATO RAGÙ

35–40
TOTAL

Preparation 20
Cooking 15–20
Serves 2

This fish dish is fragrant, fresh and extremely simple to prepare. You can, of course, use dried lentils to make this recipe and it will only add about 15 minutes to the cooking time, but when you can buy them already cooked and you've had a long day, why bother? If you've got 10 minutes free the day before, there is plenty in this recipe that can be done in advance to make things easier when you come home the following night. Halibut is a meaty, silky smooth fish that is very forgiving to cook and very satisfying to eat. It is great for a special occasion or just when you feel like spoiling yourself.

For the ragù
300g cooked Puy lentils
2 teaspoons Dijon mustard
1 red onion, peeled and chopped
100g sunblush tomatoes, chopped
2 sprigs of thyme, leaves only, chopped
zest and juice of 2 lemons
50ml extra virgin olive oil
salt and freshly ground black pepper

a small bunch of flatleaf parsley, chopped

For the halibut
2 tablespoons olive oil
2 boneless halibut fillets, weighing
  150–180g each
juice of ½ lemon
2 tablespoons pesto or chermoula sauce
  (see page 48), to serve

1 For the ragù, pour the cooked lentils into a small saucepan. Place on a low heat and add the Dijon mustard, red onion, sunblush tomatoes (including their juices), thyme, lemon zest and juice and the olive oil. Season with salt and pepper and heat for 5–6 minutes to allow all the flavours to infuse. Once the ragù is warmed through, remove it from the heat and add the chopped parsley. Leave to cool.

2 Now you can cook the fish. Heat the olive oil in a frying pan and add the fish, skin-side down. Season the fish on the flesh side, reduce the heat and cook for about 8 minutes (depending on the thickness of the fish), until the underside is golden brown. Then turn the fish over and pour over the lemon juice. Turn the heat off and let the residual heat in the pan finish off the cooking. The fish can also be grilled if you prefer (cook for 4–5 minutes on each side).

3 When the fish has cooked through and you are ready to serve, place a large spoonful of the cooled lentil ragù onto each plate. Lay the fish on top of the ragù and top off with a spoonful of pesto or chermoula sauce.

If you don't like fish try this dish with a plump chicken breast. Cook the chicken on the skin side to ensure a lovely crispy finish.

RUMP STEAK WITH BLUE CHEESE BUTTER

25

TOTAL

Preparation 15

Cooking 10

plus 5 minutes
resting time

Serves 2

The best things in life are often the simplest! Need I say more?

For the blue cheese butter
75g unsalted butter, cut into cubes
**75g good strong blue cheese like a Stilton
or Roquefort**
zest of 1 lemon
2 tablespoons chopped parsley
salt and freshly ground black pepper

For the steaks
2 good-quality rump steaks, weighing
**about 200–250g each (aged for at least
28 days if possible)**
2 tablespoons olive oil

To serve
a bunch of watercress
juice of 1 lemon
2 tablespoons olive oil
**baked potatoes or Chunky Potato Wedges,
see page 123 (optional)**

1 First make the butter. Place all the butter, except for two cubes, in a blender along with the blue cheese, lemon zest and parsley. Season with pepper and blitz until everything is combined. Tip the contents into a bowl and set aside.

2 Season the steaks on both sides. Pour the olive oil into a hot frying pan and lay in the steaks. Don't move the steaks around too much. A 3cm-thick steak will need around 5 minutes per side for the steak to be cooked medium. Once the steak has had its first 5 minutes, drop in the cubes of the remaining butter and turn the steak, you should see lots of caramelisation – this is very important for the flavour of the finished dish.

3 While the steaks are cooking, make sure you keep spooning the butter in the pan over them so they stay nice and juicy. When cooked, take them out of the pan and allow them to rest for at least 5 minutes. If you don't do this, all the work will be for nothing and your steaks will be tough.

4 To serve, place the steaks on your serving plates and add a big spoonful of the blue cheese butter. Dress the watercress leaves with the lemon juice and olive oil and serve on the side together with either a jacket potato or the Chunky Potato Wedges if you wish.

**This dish is
great followed
by a Tiramisu
(see page 162).**

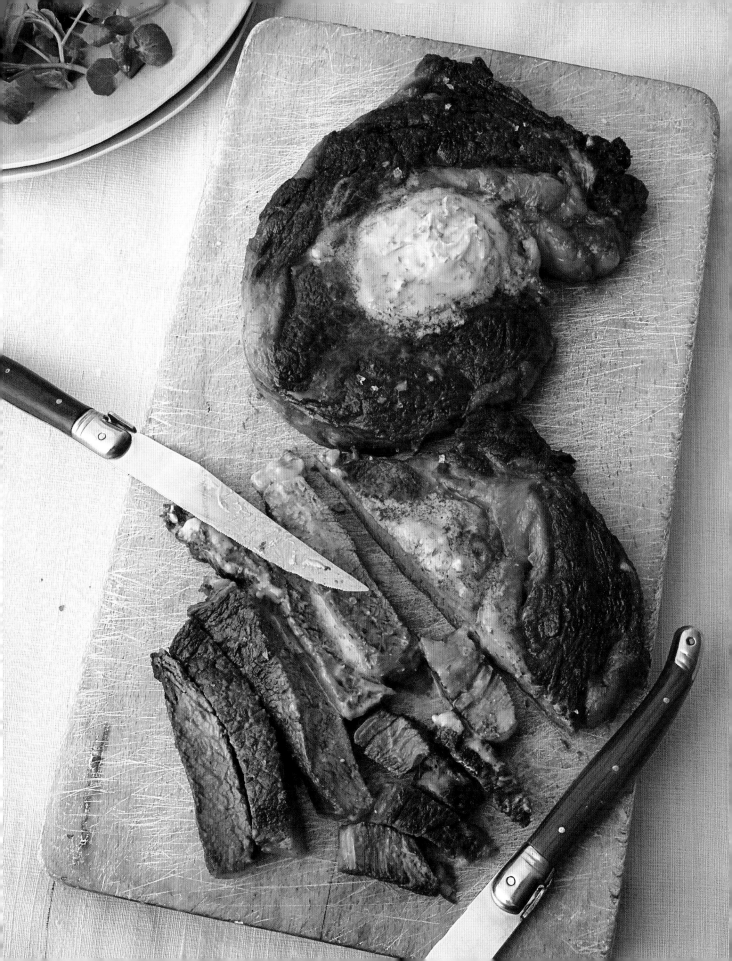

WHITE CRAB AND GREEN APPLE COCKTAIL WITH AVOCADO AND LIME PURÉE

15
___
TOTAL

Preparation 15
Cooking 0
Serves 4

This is a really elegant little starter, lovely and light and ideal for entertaining in summer. You can serve it a few ways, either as a little canapé on toasted bruschetta, or in a cocktail glass for a more robust starter. I thinks it's great both ways and if you only served this to me, I'd be very happy indeed.

For the crab and apple cocktail
2 Granny Smith apples, skin left on and grated or cut into thin matchsticks
400g picked white crabmeat
1 tablespoon soured cream
½ small bunch of chives, snipped
a small handful of basil leaves, chopped
zest and juice of 2 limes

For the avocado and lime purée
2 avocados

zest and juice of 1 lime
1 small red chilli, deseeded and chopped
2 tablespoons soured cream
salt and freshly ground black pepper
olive oil (optional)

To serve
2 Little Gem lettuces, finely sliced
1 lime
chives or chervil, to garnish (optional)

1 As soon as you have grated the apples, put all the crab and apple cocktail ingredients into a bowl and mix together with a wooden spoon to stop the apples from browning.

2 Place all the ingredients for the avocado purée into a food-processor and season with salt and pepper. Whizz thoroughly – if the mixture gets a bit stuck add a glug of olive oil to help it on its way. It should be as smooth as possible.

3 If you are serving this in glasses, put a small amount of the sliced Little Gem at the bottom of each one along with a squeeze of lime juice. Spoon 2–3 tablespoons of the avocado purée on top and then evenly distribute the crab mix. Garnish with a chive or some chervil, if you have it.

Serve as a starter before the Rump Steak with Blue Cheese Butter (see page 88) or the Clams and Smoky Bacon (see page 97).

SEARED DUCK BREAST WITH WATERCRESS, CASHEWS AND POMEGRANATE

30

TOTAL

Preparation 10

Cooking 20

Serves 4

or 6–8 as a starter

This light dish is best served at room temperature and therefore perfect for a summer evening. It takes hardly any time to prepare and the only thing that actually needs cooking is the duck.

For the dressing
zest of 2 oranges
juice of 1 lemon
6 tablespoons olive oil
a pinch of ground cinnamon
a pinch of ground cumin
1 teaspoon balsamic vinegar
1 tablespoon Dijon mustard

1 teaspoon runny honey

For the duck
4 duck breasts, skin on
100g cashew nuts
1 pomegranate or 1 x 100g packet
   pre-picked pomegranate seeds
300g watercress, big stalks removed

1 Preheat the oven to 180°C/350°F/Gas 4. To make the dressing, place all the ingredients into a glass jar, tightly screw on the lid and shake hard until all the ingredients have combined. Set the 2 zested oranges aside for the duck.

2 Make four or five light slashes in the fat of the duck breast. Rub 2 tablespoons of dressing from the jar into the duck breasts. Place an ovenproof frying pan on the stove, turn on the heat to medium and lay in the duck breasts. It's better to start cooking the duck in a cold pan so the fat can melt and the marinade won't burn. Cook the duck skin-side down for 6–8 minutes. Keep checking that the marinade isn't catching.

3 While the duck is cooking, cut off the top and bottom of the zested oranges. Using a small serrated knife remove the outer peel and pith. Cut the segments from the orange by holding it in your hand, cutting in between each membrane and pushing out the juicy segment. Let the segments fall into a clean bowl. Squeeze out any remaining juice into the duck pan.

4 Turn the duck over and finish cooking in the oven for a further 5 minutes for pink meat and 10 minutes for well done. Remove from the oven and leave to rest.

5 Spread the cashew nuts over a baking tray and toast in the oven for 5 minutes or until golden brown.

When blood oranges are in season use them if possible.

6 Mix the pomegranate seeds with the orange segments. Pour over half the dressing, mix in the cashews and watercress and pile high on plates or a large platter. Slice the duck and place on top of the salad. Drizzle over the remaining dressing and serve.

BAKED SKATE WING WITH ROASTED ARTICHOKES, OLIVES AND CAPERS

25

TOTAL

Preparation 10

Cooking 15

Serves 4

Try the roasted artichokes, capers and olives with some parboiled baby new potatoes to make a great side dish to go with chicken or pork.

Skate is a highly underused fish that has great texture and is extremely easy to cook. I find that it is also a really good choice of fish to start non-fish lovers on. Unlike other fish, it has big cartilage-type bones that the meat pulls away from with ease. This is an all-in-one-pan dish, so there's not too much washing up and hardly any preparation needed. What could be better?

4 skate wings, weighing about 125–175g each
300g marinated artichokes, drained (try to buy the pre-roasted ones in oil)
3 tablespoons black olives
salt and freshly ground black pepper
2 tablespoons olive oil

40g butter
100ml white wine
4 tablespoons capers in vinegar

To serve
2 tablespoons chopped parsley
boiled new potatoes

1 Preheat the oven to 200°C/400°F/Gas 6. Lay the skate wings onto a roasting tray (you may need to divide the ingredients between 2 trays depending on the size of the wings). Scatter over the artichokes and olives. Season with a few pinches of salt and lots of black pepper. Drizzle over the olive oil, dot the butter over the fish and pour over the white wine.

2 Put the tray in the oven for 10 minutes, then remove and scatter over the capers. Return to the oven for another 5 minutes.

3 Remove the tray from the oven and sprinkle on the chopped parsley. Serve at the table with some new potatoes.

CLAMS AND SMOKY BACON

25

TOTAL

Preparation 10

Cooking 15

Serves 2

or 4 as a starter

Try seving with the White Crab and Green Apple Cocktail to start (see page 91), or follow with the Almond, Hazelnut and Vanilla Biscuits (see page 147).

This is the perfect quick dinner for a special night. I know clams are easy to come by in most supermarkets now, but I still get really excited about cooking them. They will always remind me of family holidays to the south of France when I was little and I would spend hours picking the lovely juicy meat out of the tiny shells. My top tip is to always buy more clams than you think you're going to eat because, trust me, you'll want to go back for more.

2 tablespoons olive oil
150g smoked bacon rashers or smoked pancetta, chopped into fine strips
2 shallots, peeled and chopped
¼ teaspoon chilli flakes
1 bay leaf
2 garlic cloves, peeled and chopped
50g butter
125ml double cream

2kg cleaned clams
125ml Vermouth or dry white wine
freshly ground black pepper

To serve
1 lemon, cut into wedges
extra virgin olive oil, to drizzle
crusty bread

1 Heat the oil in a large saucepan and add the bacon, shallots, chilli flakes and bay leaf. Sweat them gently for 4–5 minutes, until soft, before adding the garlic and the butter. Allow the butter to melt before adding the double cream.

2 Increase the heat and allow the cream to boil for 2 minutes, then add the clams and Vermouth or white wine. Season well with pepper, stir and put on a tight-fitting lid.

3 Let the clams cook for 5 minutes, shaking the pan hard halfway through. Once all the clams are open, serve straight away with a wedge of lemon, a drizzle of olive oil and a big chunk of crusty bread to soak up all the juices.

RED WINE, GORGONZOLA AND ORANGE RISOTTO

30
TOTAL

Preparation 10
Cooking 20
Serves 4
or 6–8 as a starter

It's not often that I make risotto, but when I do I need it to be interesting so I like to bulk out the rice with a full-bodied red wine, nuts and a tasty strong cheese. There's always a different flavour in each mouthful. This is my favourite risotto so far – it's simple yet so full of flavour and also works well as a starter.

1.5 litres chicken or vegetable stock
2 tablespoons olive oil
75g butter
2 shallots, peeled and chopped
350g risotto rice
200ml red wine

salt and freshly ground black pepper
zest of 2 oranges
200g Gorgonzola
100g Parmesan cheese, grated, plus extra
  to serve (optional)
100g crushed walnuts (optional)

1 Place the stock in a saucepan and bring to the boil.

2 Place a large shallow pan on the stove and turn the heat to medium. Add the olive oil and half the butter. When the butter has melted, add the shallots and cook for 3 minutes until soft. Once soft, add in the rice grains and stir around in the butter and oil until all the grains are coated.

3 Increase the heat to full and add the red wine. Stir the grains around in the wine continuously until all the wine has been absorbed. Then start gradually adding the stock, a ladleful at a time. Never stop gently stirring the risotto. Once one ladleful of stock has been absorbed, add the next. Season with a big pinch of salt and pepper.

4 When the rice is nearly cooked (after about 14 minutes of stirring), add the orange zest. Add another ladle of stock then crumble in the Gorgonzola and stir well so all the cheese melts. Taste for seasoning – you will quite likely need more pepper.

5 When the rice is cooked to al dente, add the remaining butter and the Parmesan cheese. Stir through and serve with extra Parmesan and crushed walnuts, if you wish.

A full-bodied red wine works best for this risotto so buy the strongest you can to get maximum flavour.

ROASTED QUAIL AND FIGS STUFFED WITH GOAT'S CHEESE AND HONEY WITH A PICKLED WALNUT DRESSING

35

TOTAL

Preparation 10

Cooking 25

Serves 2

or 4 as a starter

You can find quails in most good supermarkets all year round. I can't help but buy them and I've never had a displeased diner when I've cooked up this starter for them. It's quite big and, of course, can also be eaten as a main course, but I tend to go with a light main if I cook this at a dinner party. Serve quails slightly pink and they go particularly well with the sweet/salty duo of goat's cheese and fig. They are easy to prepare and, as they are so small, this dish cooks in no time.

6 large ripe figs
200g goat's cheese
4 whole quails
salt and freshly ground black pepper
olive oil, for roasting
2 tablespoons runny honey
Lamb's lettuce, mache or pea tops, to serve

For the pickled walnut dressing
6 pickled walnuts, roughly chopped
1 tablespoon Dijon mustard
2 tablespoons sticky balsamic vinegar
1 tablespoon chopped parsley
4 tablespoons olive oil

1 Preheat the oven to 200°C/400°F/Gas. Cut the figs criss-cross style from the top to halfway down and push up from the bottom to open them up like a flower. Push as much goat's cheese into the opening of the fig as you can – be very generous.

2 Season the quails with salt and pepper and place on a baking tray along with the figs. Drizzle both the quails and the figs with the olive oil and the runny honey and put in the oven to roast for 12–15 minutes.

3 Meanwhile, make a dressing by mixing the pickled walnuts with the mustard, vinegar, chopped parsley and olive oil.

4 After 15 minutes, remove the tray from the oven, take out the figs and set aside. Return the quails to the oven for a further 10 minutes.

5 Serve 1 quail and 1 fig per person, garnish with a handful of lamb's lettuce or mache and drizzle with the pickled walnut dressing. You can carve the meat from the quail for presentation purposes if you prefer by removing both the legs, cutting down the breastbone and removing both breasts.

Most game goes really with figs – try this dish with a pan-fried pigeon breast.

PAN-FRIED MONKFISH WITH WILD MUSHROOMS, CARAMELISED ONIONS AND A HERBY SOURED CREAM SAUCE

30
TOTAL

Preparation 10
Cooking 20
Serves 2

Monkfish is a really meaty fish that holds up well to big bold flavours. It's a great fish to serve to non-fish-loving guests and is also very easy and forgiving to cook. It won't fall apart like some fish but you can of course overcook it, so be careful to cook gently until perfectly cooked through. Mushrooms are my number one choice of accompaniment with sweet onions.

For the onions
20g butter
1 tablespoon olive oil
3 large onions, peeled and finely sliced
100ml white wine
1 tablespoon caster sugar
1 tablespoon white wine vinegar

For the monkfish
50g butter
2 garlic cloves, peeled and chopped

4 sprigs of thyme, leaves only
2 monkfish fillets, weighing about 150g each
100ml white wine
250g wild mushrooms or a selection pack of mixed mushrooms, the large ones sliced
a bunch of flatleaf parsley, chopped
1 lemon, cut in half
salt and freshly ground black pepper
100ml soured cream

1 To caramelise the onions, heat the butter and oil in a saucepan, add the onions and allow them to sweat for 5–6 minutes. Add the white wine, sugar and vinegar and cook for 10–15 minutes until all the liquid has evaporated and the onions are soft and sweet. Keep them moving in the pan to ensure they don't burn.

2 Meanwhile, heat up a large frying pan and add the butter, garlic and thyme leaves. Add the monkfish and colour for about 2 minutes on each side until golden. Add a drop of oil if the butter starts to burn. Cook for a further 2 minutes, then add the wine and cook for a further 3 minutes.

3 Move the monkfish to one side, add the mushrooms and cook for 2–3 minutes until they are wilted. Add half of the fresh parsley, the juice of half the lemon, a big pinch of salt and lots of black pepper. Meanwhile, make the herby soured cream sauce by heating the soured cream in a small pan with the remaining parsley and the juice of the other half of the lemon.

4 Serve the onions with the fish and the mushrooms. You can serve the soured cream sauce on the side or on top of the fish.

Any meaty fish works well with this recipe – brill or halibut are both great. For something completely different try using veal.

CRAB LINGUINE

25
TOTAL

Preparation 10
Cooking 15
Serves 4

This is simply the most satisfying quick dish that I can think of. I absolutely love crab and although it is quite expensive, it is such a special product that should be treated with the utmost respect. Crab speaks for itself so needs very little doing to it.

salt
500g dried linguine pasta
3 tablespoons olive oil
1 banana shallot, peeled and finely diced
2 red chillies, deseeded and finely chopped
a pinch of chilli flakes
3 garlic cloves, peeled and sliced

125ml white wine
75g butter
16–20 cherry tomatoes, halved
juice of 1 large lemon
350g picked white crabmeat
½ bunch of flatleaf parsley, finely chopped

1 Put a big pan of water on the stove to boil and add a pinch of salt. When the water starts to boil, add the pasta and cook as described on the packet until al dente.

2 In a separate pan, pour in the olive oil and turn to a medium heat. Add the shallot, chillies, chilli flakes and garlic. Allow to sweat for a few minutes in the olive oil (make sure the garlic does not burn). Add the white wine and the butter and bring to the boil to burn off the alcohol. Add the cherry tomatoes, lemon juice and white crabmeat.

3 Once the pasta is cooked, drain, reserving a couple of tablespoons of the cooking liquor. Mix the pasta into the crab sauce along with the reserved cooking liquor from the pasta. Stir through the parsley and serve.

As this is so quick to make, why not spend another few minutes making Blueberry Pie for pudding (see page 152)?

COD AND PAPRIKA CHOWDER

45

TOTAL

Preparation 15
Cooking 30
Serves 4
as a light
main course

A chowder is a lovely thick soup that works well as a starter or main course. My recipe for chowder is quite meaty so I tend to serve it as a main course, but a nice alternative is to omit the fish and make the dish a little lighter. The base to a good chowder is very important, so follow the recipe closely and it will be fabulous.

500ml semi-skimmed milk
1 fish stock cube
550g cod (or haddock or pollock), skinned
1 bay leaf
100g butter
150g smoked pancetta, diced
1 leek, trimmed and white part finely diced
300g butternut squash, peeled and finely diced into 1cm pieces

2 garlic cloves, peeled and chopped
1 teaspoon smoked paprika
100ml Vermouth or white wine
3 tablespoons plain flour
1 tablespoon chopped parsley
juice of 1 lemon
freshly ground black pepper
1 x 200g tin sweetcorn
crackers, to serve (optional)

1 Put the milk into a large saucepan, crumble in the stock cube and add the fish and bay leaf. Turn the heat to medium and bring the milk to a simmer. Remove from the heat, carefully lift out the fish onto a plate and set aside the cooking liquor for later.

2 Melt half of the butter in another saucepan on a medium heat and add the pancetta. Cook for a few minutes before adding the leek, butternut squash, garlic and smoked paprika. Soften for a few minutes before adding the Vermouth or white wine. Cook for about 10 minutes until all the ingredients are tender, then remove everything from the pan and set aside.

3 Melt the remaining butter in the same pan. Add the flour and mix to form a paste. Cook for 3 minutes, always moving the paste around in the pan, and then gradually add the reserved cooking liquor from the fish in three or four batches. Mix constantly to remove any floury lumps. Allow the mix to boil in between adding the next lot of liquid. If the soup looks too thick (it should be the consistency of runny yogurt), just add a little water.

Try using smoked cod or haddock as an alternative.

4 Flake the cod into the chowder, leaving it as chunky as possible, and then add the cooked vegetables, sweetcorn and any juices. Stir in the parsley and season with lemon juice and pepper. Crumble over some crackers if using.

FRIED SQUID WITH CHORIZO, FETA AND CHICKPEA SALAD

25

TOTAL

Preparation 15

Cooking 10

Serves 2

or 4 as a starter

Squid is one of those ingredients that needs to be either cooked quickly or long and slowly. I personally prefer the quick method as I tend to be quite impatient, which makes this the ideal meal to cook after coming home from work when you need something pronto.

For the salad
1 x 400g tin chickpeas
75g pitted black olives, roughly chopped
2 garlic cloves, peeled and finely grated
1 red onion, trimmed and thinly sliced
a small bunch of flatleaf parsley, chopped
100g feta
1 tablespoon sherry vinegar
2 tablespoons olive oil
salt and freshly ground black pepper
100g rocket

For the squid
12 cleaned squid tubes
2 teaspoons olive oil
150g chorizo, cut into slices
1 teaspoon smoked paprika
juice of 1 lemon
a sprig of oregano, leaves only, finely
 chopped
crusty bread, to serve

1 To make the chickpea salad, drain the chickpeas and place in a large mixing bowl. Add the olives, garlic, onion and parsley. Crumble in the feta and mix well. Pour over the sherry vinegar and olive oil and season with salt and pepper.

2 To prepare the squid, slit the cleaned tubes in half so they open like a book. Gently score the inside of the flesh in a criss-cross pattern with a sharp knife then cut into 3 pieces. This will help the squid cook quicker and make it more tender.

3 Heat up a frying pan, add the olive oil and allow it to get hot. Add the chorizo to the pan and cook for 3–4 minutes to allow the fat to render out of the chorizo. When that starts to happen, increase the heat and add the squid along with the smoked paprika. Cook for 3–4 minutes, then add the lemon juice, salt and pepper and the oregano.

4 Pour the cooked squid and chorizo into the salad and mix in the rocket. Serve with crusty bread.

This dish also makes a great starter followed by Rump Steak with Blue Cheese Butter (see page 88).

SEARED TUNA WITH GRAPEFRUIT, CHILLI AND BASIL SALSA

25

TOTAL

Preparation 20

Cooking 5

Serves 2

This recipe makes a great light main course and creates very little mess and stress. I've also served this as a starter before a heavy main course when I serve three or four slices of the rare seared tuna and a spoonful of the salsa. It's light, healthy and very refreshing.

cracked black pepper and salt
2 x 125g tuna steaks
olive oil, to drizzle

For the salsa
1 whole grapefruit
3 large plum tomatoes

6 spring onions
1 large red chilli, seeds in, finely chopped
salt and freshly ground black pepper
a pinch of sugar
zest and juice of 1 lime
2 tablespoons extra virgin olive oil
a handful of basil leaves

1 Make the salsa by segmenting the grapefruit and cutting the segments into four pieces. Cut the tomatoes into quarters and remove all the seeds and pulp. Now cut each petal into four strips and mix with the grapefruit. Finely slice the spring onions, including the green part, and add to the salsa mixture. Mix in the red chilli, leaving the seeds in for a bit of a kick if you fancy. Season with salt, pepper and a pinch of sugar and add the lime juice and zest alongside a couple of tablespoons of olive oil. (You can leave the salsa to stand overnight if you have time.)

2 Heat a frying pan or griddle pan until it starts to smoke. Season the tuna steaks with salt and pepper and rub with a little oil. Lay the fish into the pan and sear for 1–2 minutes on each side, depending on how you like it cooked. Remove from the pan and leave to cool.

3 Once the tuna is rested cut into 4–5 thin slices. Add the basil leaves to the salsa – either roughly tear them or leave whole if they are small. Serve the fish with a big spoonful of the salsa on the side.

Try following with The Dreaded Soufflé for dessert (see page 150).

SEA BASS WITH A FENNEL, ORANGE, PINE NUT AND SULTANA SALAD

This is surprisingly fast to prepare and looks colourful and interesting on the plate so is guaranteed to impress. It's got a very Mediterranean feel, so is ideal for a summer's eve or as a light main course after a larger starter.

25
TOTAL

Preparation 15
Cooking 10
Serves 4

2 large oranges
75g sultanas
4 fennel bulbs, trimmed and very finely sliced
100g toasted pine nuts (blanched whole almonds are also very nice)

a small bunch of dill, roughly chopped
juice of 2 lemons
1 tablespoon extra virgin olive oil
salt and freshly ground black pepper
1 tablespoon vegetable oil
4 large sea bass fillets, pin-boned

1 Cut the top and bottom off the oranges and remove all the outer skin and pith using a small serrated knife. Remove the orange segments and put them into a large mixing bowl. Pour any juice caught in the bowl into a small saucepan, add the sultanas and place on a very low heat until the juice boils. Remove from the heat and leave to cool.

2 Add the fennel, toasted pine nuts and dill to the orange segments. Pour over the cooled sultanas and orange juice, half the lemon juice and the olive oil. Season to taste.

3 Put a frying pan on a medium heat and add the vegetable oil. Season the fish and, when the oil is hot, lay the fillets skin-side down in the pan. Cook for 3–4 minutes before turning the fish over and pouring over half of the remaining lemon juice. Turn off the heat and leave the fish to finish cooking in the residual heat for a further 3 minutes.

4 Serve straight away with the crispy fennel salad.

If you're craving something sweet try the Berry Gratin (see page 148) to finish off this meal.

VEAL CHOP WITH MUSTARD MASH AND A MADEIRA AND MUSHROOM SAUCE

35

TOTAL

Preparation 15
Cooking 20
Serves 2

I just love veal and if you're a sensible shopper and buy rose veal, which has been reared in a humane way, eating veal is absolutely fine. It goes so well with this mustard mash and the Madeira sauce is a must.

3 large potatoes, peeled and cut into 3cm chunks
2 garlic cloves, peeled and left whole
salt and freshly ground black pepper
75ml double cream
95g butter
1 tablespoon wholegrain mustard
1 tablespoon olive oil
2 veal chops on the bone

For the Madeira and mushroom sauce
200g chestnut mushrooms (or wild mushrooms if they are in season), sliced
20g butter
2 sprigs of thyme, leaves only
100ml Madeira wine
100ml double cream
juice of ½ lemon

1 Put the potatoes into a saucepan, cover with water, add the garlic and a big pinch of salt and bring to the boil. Cook for about 20 minutes until tender and then drain. Heat the cream with 75g of the butter in a small pan and mash the potatoes really well. Gradually add the hot cream and butter, to the mashed potatoes, mix in the mustard and season well.

2 While the potatoes are cooking, heat a large frying pan with the olive oil and remaining butter. Season the chops on both sides with salt and pepper and lay into the oil. Cook for 6–7 minutes on each side (depending on the thickness) until golden brown. The chops should be served pink. Keep spooning the pan juices over them as they cook to keep them moist. When cooked, remove from the pan and leave to rest.

3 To make the sauce, add the mushrooms to the pan along with the butter and thyme. Sweat for 1 minute before adding the Madeira wine and double cream. Bring to the boil, season with salt and pepper and add the lemon juice.

4 Serve the mash with the chop on the side and a good spoonful of the mushroom sauce.

To make a really smooth mash, I like to use a ricer – this is the best way I know to ensure there are no lumps.

Tuck In

Not every night has to be a sit-down dinner. One of the best ways to enjoy food and the company of others is by laying out a big spread and letting everyone tuck in. You might be celebrating or catching up with friends, having the family over and don't have enough chairs for everyone to sit on, or just want something really informal where everyone can feel relaxed. My favourite is a night with the girls where we can all really eat our fill, but I know many mums, wives and girlfriends who will cook this type of food for the kids after school or as a quick snack for the other important people in their lives. Dinners don't always have to be eaten with a knife and fork sitting around a perfectly laid table. This is good, wholesome food that can be set out ready for people to pick from, making your life a whole lot simpler.

HOMEMADE CHICKEN AND HALLOUMI SHISH

30
TOTAL

Preparation **15**
Cooking **15**
plus marinating time
Serves **4**

I regularly feed this to friends after a night out or when I wasn't expecting company as I tend to have all the basics stocked in my fridge most of the time. Don't even think about making this dish unless you have a hot chilli sauce in your cupboard – it's just not the same without it.

15 mini chicken fillets
1 x 200g block halloumi cheese, cut into
   12 cubes
1 lemon, cut into wedges

For the marinade
1 red chilli, finely chopped
2 garlic cloves, peeled and grated or finely
   chopped
grated zest and juice of 1 lemon
4 tablespoons olive oil
1 tablespoon ground cumin
1 teaspoon ground coriander

salt and freshly ground black pepper

For the pittas
4 large pitta breads
½ small white cabbage, shredded
1 red onion, peeled and finely sliced
2 large plum tomatoes, sliced
¼ cucumber, sliced
200g houmous
4 tablespoons Greek yogurt
4 large pickled chillies (not too hot)
½ bunch of coriander
hot chilli sauce, to serve

1 Put the chicken and halloumi into a large mixing bowl and add the marinade ingredients. Cover and set aside to marinate.

2 Preheat the grill to hot or heat a griddle. Skewer the chicken and the halloumi onto metal skewers or wooden ones that have been soaked in water for a few minutes to stop them burning. You should have three pieces of halloumi on each skewer.

3 Lay the skewers under the grill or on the griddle and cook for 6 minutes. Turn the skewers over and cook for a further 6 minutes. Squeeze over the juice of quarter of a lemon.

4 Heat up the pittas either in a toaster or under the grill. Cut down the middle of the pitta with a sharp knife and make a pocket. Pull the chicken and halloumi off the skewers into a bowl. Have the salad ingredients laid out in front of you.

5 Spread the inside of the pittas generously with houmous before loading in the salad, more lemon juice and finally the chicken and halloumi. Spoon a dollop of Greek yogurt on each pitta and lay across a chilli, tear over some coriander and serve with a good dollop of hot chilli sauce.

If you are serving these to bigger numbers, you could put all the salad and accompaniments in the middle of the table and let your guests build their shish themselves.

ROSIE'S VEGAN CURRY (THE BOYS NEVER KNEW!)

45–50
TOTAL

Preparation 10
Cooking 35–40
Serves 6–8

My wonderful cousin Rosie recently became a vegan. A horrible thought for us meat lovers, but an exciting challenge for a chef like me to have to come up with a recipe to not only serve to her, but also my boyfriend and his meat-loving friends who had just returned from a bad football game and would need some serious cheering up with a decent hearty meal.

2 tablespoons vegetable oil
2 large onions, peeled and finely chopped
3 large green chillies, chopped
5cm piece of fresh ginger, peeled and finely chopped
4 garlic cloves, peeled and finely chopped
3 teaspoons ground cumin
2 teaspoons ground coriander
2 teaspoons chilli powder
2 teaspoons turmeric
2 tablespoons tomato purée
salt
1 cinnamon stick
2 x 400g tins chopped tomatoes

2 x 400g tins cooked green lentils
1 butternut squash, cut into 2cm dice (no need to peel, just remove the seeds)
1 cauliflower, cut into small florets
100g green beans, cut into thirds
a large bunch of coriander, roughly chopped
juice of 1 lemon

To serve
rice or naan breads and natural yogurt or raita

1 Heat a heavy-based pan on a medium heat. Add the oil to the pan and the onions, chillies, ginger and garlic. Cook for 4–5 minutes until the onions start to soften and go translucent.

2 Add all the dried spices and coat the onion mixture well. Cook for a further 4–5 minutes before adding the tomato purée, a good pinch of salt and the cinnamon stick. Stir well. Add the tinned tomatoes and lentils, reduce the heat and leave the sauce to simmer for 10 minutes.

3 Add the vegetables, starting with those that take longer to cook. First add the butternut squash and cook for 10–15 minutes, then add the cauliflower and cook for a further 15–20 minutes. Add about 125ml of water at this stage if the stew is looking a little dry. Allow the mix to boil.

4 Just before serving, add the green beans and cook until just tender. Then add the coriander. Taste for seasoning and add the lemon juice. Stir well before serving with either rice or naan bread and natural yogurt or raita on the side.

To make sure this meal is vegan-friendly use soya yogurt to serve.

BARBECUE CHINESE RIBS

40
TOTAL

Preparation 10
Cooking 30
Serves 8

We all love barbecued ribs and this is a great recipe that can also be used on chicken. You don't have to marinate the meat as it's a thick sauce and will stick and caramelise as the meat cooks. This really is great finger food for a relaxed evening.

2 red chillies, finely chopped
2.5cm piece of fresh ginger, peeled and finely chopped
3 garlic cloves, peeled and finely chopped
100ml soy sauce
3 tablespoons honey
2 tablespoons dark soft brown sugar
2 tablespoons tomato purée
3 tablespoons tomato ketchup

1 tablespoon red wine vinegar
2 tablespoons vegetable oil
a large pinch of salt
20 pork ribs

To serve
1 red chilli, sliced
2 spring onions, trimmed and sliced

1 Preheat the oven to 180°C/350°F/Gas 4. Make the marinade by combining all the ingredients, except for the pork ribs, in a food-processor. Whizz to a fine paste.

2 Pour half of the sauce over the ribs in a shallow, ovenproof container and rub in well. Put in the oven and cook the pork ribs for 30 minutes (or 25 minutes if using chicken wings). Check regularly to see if the sauce is burning a little too much or drying out – if this happens, pour in a couple of tablespoons of water.

3 Pour the remaining sauce into a saucepan and boil for 3–4 minutes to heat the sauce for dipping the ribs. Remove the saucepan from the heat and set aside.

4 Once the meat is cooked, transfer the ribs to a chopping board. Use a sharp knife to cut in between each rib to carve them into individual portions. If you wish you can transfer to plates, spoon over the sauce and sprinkle the chilli and spring onions on top. This dish is perfect with some sticky rice on the side.

This marinade has many uses – it's great just as a dip or smothered over chicken wings.

BREADED SCAMPI AND TARTARE SAUCE

35

TOTAL

Preparation 20

Cooking 15

Serves 8

I love the sort of food you can carry through in a basket and let everyone dig into. No airs and graces here, ladies and gentlemen! Just pick it up, dunk it and enjoy. Watch out, though... they'll be hot!

For the tartare sauce
2 eggs, separated
1 teaspoon Dijon mustard
300ml vegetable oil
salt and freshly ground black pepper
juice of 1/2 lemon
2 teaspoons capers
1 tablespoon baby gherkins

For the scampi
1 litre vegetable oil, for deep-frying
  (optional)
100g plain flour
2 large eggs
200g dried breadcrumbs
30 raw large prawns, peeled
2 lemons, cut into wedges, to serve

1 If you plan to cook your scampi in the oven, preheat it to 200°C/400°F/Gas 6. First make the tartare sauce. Put the egg yolks into a blender or a bowl with the Dijon mustard (reserve the egg whites for the scampi). Whisk or blitz together well before very slowly adding the oil, drop by drop. You can speed up the process once the mixture starts to thicken. Once thickened to the consistency of mayonnaise, season with salt and pepper and add the lemon juice. Blitz in the capers and gherkins so they are small but still chunky. Chop them by hand and mix in if you're not using a blender.

2 If you are deep-frying your scampi, put the oil in the fryer or a wide, deep pan and fill no more than halfway. Turn the heat to medium.

3 Put the flour, eggs and egg whites and the breadcrumbs into three separate bowls. Beat the eggs together and season the flour. Dry the prawns and pass first through the flour, then the egg, and then the breadcrumbs. Coat well.

4 If cooking in the oven, put the breaded prawns straight onto a baking tray and bake for 10–15 minutes until golden brown. Turn them once during cooking.

5 If deep-frying, check the oil temperature by dropping in a pinch of breadcrumbs. If they sizzle and rise to the top, the oil is ready. Cook the prawns in batches of about 5–6 at a time. Place the prawns onto a large slotted spoon and gently lower into the oil. Move them around until they are golden brown, which will take about 2–4 minutes. Remove from the oil and lay on kitchen paper to drain while you cook the rest.

6 Season with salt and serve with wedges of lemon and the tartare sauce.

For a night of nibbles serve alongside the Deep-fried Mozzarella Balls with Jalapeño Cheese Dip (see page 134).

LEMONGRASS STEAMED PRAWNS

25–26
TOTAL

Preparation 20
Cooking 5–6
Serves 4

If you are
serving this
dish as a main
course steam
some jasmine
rice and serve
it on the side.

This is a traditional way of cooking prawns in Thailand, a place very close to my heart and one of my favourite methods of cookery. Your dinner will be packed full of flavour as well as looking very pretty on the plate or platter. This recipe is ideal for finger food at a little party or gathering or as a nice light main course at a dinner party.

24 raw large prawns, peeled
4 sticks of lemongrass, first 2 layers peeled
  off to make the stick into a spear
5cm piece of fresh ginger, peeled and cut
  into fine strips
½ green chilli, finely sliced
2 tablespoons light soy sauce

1 teaspoon Thai fish sauce
juice of 1 lime
1 teaspoon caster sugar
4 spring onions, trimmed and sliced
Thai Dipping Sauce (see page 136), to
  serve (optional)

1 Heat a saucepan of water to boiling. I like to use a traditional bamboo steamer for this dish, although an upturned saucer in the bottom of a large, deep frying pan that has a lid will also do as a makeshift steamer.

2 Spear as many of the prawns onto the lemongrass spear as you can. If the prawns are particularly big, you may need more than four lemongrass sticks.

3 Make the dressing by combining the ginger strips, chilli, soy sauce, fish sauce, lime juice and sugar in a bowl.

4 Place the prawn skewers onto a plate that fits inside your steamer and pour over the dressing. Steam for 5–6 minutes until the prawns have turned pink. Sprinkle over the sliced spring onions and serve immediately with the Thai Dipping Sauce, if using.

LAMB BURGERS AND CHUNKY POTATO WEDGES

45
TOTAL

Preparation 20
Cooking 25
Serves 6

Tell me a better thing to cook for a bunch of rowdy friends, family members or kids? These burgers are big and meaty, but with a little fresh twist. A big toasted bun, juicy meat and chunky wedges dipped and doused in mayo is really quite delicious and very indulgent – any friend would be highly impressed.

For the chunky wedges
6 large potatoes, skins left on, each cut
   into eight wedges
1 teaspoon ground cumin
1 teaspoon hot paprika
2 tablespoons olive oil
salt and freshly ground black pepper

For the burgers
800g minced lamb
1 teaspoon ground cumin
½ bunch of coriander, chopped

1 egg yolk
2 tablespoons vegetable oil
200g mozzarella cheese
6 burger bap buns

To serve (optional)
3 large plum tomatoes, sliced
1 red onion, left whole, peeled and sliced
   into rings
6 large pickled gherkins, sliced
mayonnaise
tomato ketchup

1 Preheat the oven to 190°C/375°F/Gas 5 and the grill to medium. Put the potato wedges in a bowl and mix with the cumin, paprika, oil and salt and pepper. Lay them out evenly on a baking tray and put into the oven for about 25 minutes until they are golden and cooked through.

2 For the burgers, mix the lamb, cumin, coriander and egg yolk with some salt and pepper in a bowl. Divide the mixture into six, roll into balls then flatten into patties.

3 Heat a large ovenproof frying pan on a high heat and add the vegetable oil. Lay in the burger patties and cook for 5 minutes on each side. Transfer the burgers to a baking sheet, place a layer of torn mozzarella on each one and put in the oven for 5 minutes.

4 Cut the burger buns in half and place under the grill for 2 minutes while the burgers rest, or put them in the hot oven if you don't have a separate grill. When they are slightly toasted, build the burgers with the tomatoes, onions and gherkins, if using, and serve with the crispy potato wedges and loads of mayonnaise and ketchup.

This also works really well with minced beef or even chicken – just make sure you cook it all the way through.

CHICKEN, APRICOT AND CHICKPEA TAGINE

55
___
TOTAL

Preparation 15
Cooking 40
Serves 6

Tagine is the Moroccan word for the pot that their famous fruity casseroles are cooked in. Tagines have become very popular in many restaurants and homes and this recipe is extremely easy and takes very little time and effort. I love meat and fruit served together and I think that more people should try it. This is the perfect dish when you have a full house as it is cooked all in one pot and transfers straight from the oven to the table.

4 tablespoons vegetable oil
800g diced chicken (or 10 boneless and
  skinless chicken thighs), diced into 2cm
  pieces
3 large onions, peeled and sliced
3 garlic cloves, peeled and chopped
1 teaspoon chopped fresh ginger
2 teaspoons ground cumin
1 teaspoon hot paprika
salt and freshly ground black pepper

200g ready-to-eat apricots
2 x 400g tins chickpeas, drained
2 x 400g tins chopped tomatoes
250ml chicken stock
4 tablespoons runny honey
2 strips orange zest
6–8 tablespoons pitted black olives
a bunch of fresh coriander, torn
Pomegranate and Almond Couscous (see
  page 43), to serve (optional)

You can add diced potatoes to this dish to make it more substantial instead of serving it with couscous or rice. Add to the pan while the chicken is cooking and cook for 20–25 minutes until tender.

1 Heat a large casserole dish on a medium heat and add half of the oil. Fry the pieces of chicken, in batches if necessary, for about 5–6 minutes until slightly golden. Remove from the pan and set aside.

2 Add the remaining oil to the pan and gently fry the onions, garlic and ginger for about 3–4 minutes until soft. Then add the cumin, hot paprika and salt and pepper and stir well.

3 Return the chicken to the casserole and add the apricots, chickpeas, tomatoes, stock, honey and the orange zest. Bring to the boil, then reduce the heat and allow the casserole to simmer for about 30 minutes until golden brown. Add the olives during the last 10 minutes of cooking.

4 Scatter the tagine with torn coriander and serve with the Pomegrante and Almond Couscous alongside, if using.

PORK AND PINEAPPLE SWEET AND SOUR NOODLE STIR-FRY

35

TOTAL

Preparation 25
Cooking 10
Serves 4

Sweet and sour is a takeaway classic. This is a much healthier option that ticks everyone's boxes when having a relaxed night in. Stir-fries are instant cooking that make all our lives easier, so the more interesting we can make them, the better.

500g pork fillet, cut into 2cm pieces
6 tablespoons dark soy sauce
1 teaspoon sesame seed oil
1 tablespoon rice wine vinegar
4 teaspoons cornflour
250g glass or rice noodles or straight-to-wok noodles
2 tablespoons groundnut or vegetable oil
100ml pineapple juice
1 tablespoon sweet chilli sauce
a handful of coriander, chopped
1 lime, cut into wedges

For the stir-fry
2.5cm piece of fresh ginger, peeled and finely cut into strips
2 garlic cloves, peeled and finely chopped
2 red chillies, cut into slices
2 red peppers, deseeded and cut into 2cm pieces
1 red onion, peeled and cut into 2cm pieces
6 spring onions, trimmed and cut into 2.5cm pieces
1 x 225g tin pineapple chunks in natural juice or 1 whole pineapple, cut into chunks

1 Start by marinating the pork in 2 tablespoons of the soy sauce, the sesame oil, vinegar and cornflour. Leave this to marinate while you prepare all the vegetables.

2 Soak the noodles in boiling water for 1 minute until soft. Drain and leave in cold water until later. If you are using straight-to-wok noodles leave out this step.

3 Heat a wok or large frying pan on the stove and add 1 tablespoon of the oil. Start cooking only when the wok is so hot the oil is nearly smoking. Remove the pork from the marinade with a slotted spoon (reserve the marinade for later) and carefully put it into the hot wok. Stir-fry the pork for about 2 minutes until it is nearly cooked all the way through and you have a little colour on the meat.

4 Remove the pork from the wok and add the remaining oil with the ginger, garlic and chilli. Stir for 1 minute before adding the remaining vegetables and the pineapple. Cook for a further 2–3 minutes before returning the pork to the wok along with the reserved pork marinade, the remaining 4 tablespoons soy sauce, the pineapple juice and the sweet chilli sauce. Allow the liquid to boil in the base of the wok for 3–4 minutes, stirring all the time.

5 Fold in the cooked glass or straight-to-wok noodles and scatter with the fresh coriander. Serve with a wedge of lime.

This also works well with king prawns or chicken.

MY CHOP SALAD

15

TOTAL

Preparation 15

Cooking 0

Serves 4–6

**Follow with
the Peach and
Pistachio Trifle
(see page 158).**

This is a salad that can be eaten as a starter or a main course. But it is massive and I always make way too much. I love this dish because it is great at barbecues, when you have friends over, or just when you can't make up your mind so you go for a salad that literally contains everything. There's hardly any preparation involved as most things come straight out of the packet, which makes it doubly good!

150g sunblush tomatoes (or chargrilled mixed vegetables), roughly chopped
200g marinated artichokes, quartered
8 cooked crispy bacon rashers
100g St Agur (or other blue cheese of your liking)
250g cooked chicken, shredded
100g walnuts, roughly chopped

1 x 400g tin sweetcorn, drained
1 Cos lettuce, sliced
4 tablespoons crème fraîche
1 tablespoon wholegrain mustard
juice of 1 lemon
salt and freshly ground black pepper
a large handful of basil leaves, to serve

1 Put the tomatoes and artichokes into a serving bowl. Break up the crispy bacon and crumble into the salad and then do the same with the cheese.

2 Add all the remaining ingredients and mix really well. Season with salt and pepper and garnish with torn basil leaves. Serve immediately.

EASY CHEESY FONDUE

30

TOTAL

Preparation 10

Cooking 20

Serves 4–6

as a fun snack
with a few drinks

This is a dish to be cooked on a cold night in with a bunch of friends. I don't know anyone that wouldn't be tempted by a bowl of molten cheese and a variety of yummy stuff to dip in it. I've come up with a way that even if you don't have a fondue kit, you can still have a go at creating this Swiss culinary treat. Of course I've made a few changes, but all in all it's pretty authentic. Make this dish as your guests arrive as it's something that has to be eaten as soon as it's ready for the best results. If you have a fondue kit, simply pour the melted cheese into the fondue after it has been made. Make sure the fondue bowl has been pre-warmed before adding the melted cheese mixture.

2 shallots, or 1 white onion, finely chopped
2 teaspoons white wine vinegar
150ml white wine
400g Gruyére cheese, grated
400g comte (or strong Cheddar if you can't get comte), grated
200g St Argur blue cheese or Gorgonzola, crumbled
1 tablespoon Dijon mustard or wholegrain mustard
200g cream cheese
100ml double cream
freshly ground black pepper

To serve
crusty bread (slightly stale) or croutons
cooked new potatoes (if you have leftover roast potatoes, these are great as well)
cornichon (mini gherkins or pickles)
pickled or raw cauliflower, carrots, baby turnips
salami or cured sausage, cut into chunky pieces
ham ends

1 Place a large saucepan of water on the stove and bring to the boil. Place a bowl on top of the pan to create a bain marie or water bath.

2 Put the chopped shallots or onion into a small saucepan with the vinegar and the white wine, bring to the boil and allow to reduce by half. Once reduced, pour the reduction into the bowl on top of the boiling water and add the Gruyére, comte and the blue cheese. Stir it around the pan slowly while the cheese melts. This will take around 15 minutes.

3 Once the cheese is nearly all melted, add the Dijon mustard, cream cheese, double cream and lots of black pepper. Make sure all the ingredients are well combined and melted.

4 If using a fondue kit, pour the mixture into the bowl now, if not, carefully take the bain marie to the table and let everyone dig in with the prepared bits and pieces to be dipped.

If you fancy something a bit different, try adding a splash of truffle oil – Cheesy Truffled Fondue. You'll be guaranteed to get a few oohs and ahhs.

GREEN APPLE SLAW

15

TOTAL

Preparation 15

Cooking 0

Serves 6

Perfect with the Lamb Burgers and Chunky Potato Wedges (see page 123).

I love this dish, either crammed into a burger or on the side with some freshly barbecued seafood. It is the ultimate side dish that suits any alfresco or casual dining down to a T.

For the dressing
1 tablespoon wholegrain mustard
2 lemons
150g crème fraîche
salt and freshly ground black pepper

For the apple slaw
2 tablespoons plump golden raisins
4 tablespoons warm apple juice or water
¼ white cabbage, finely shredded
2 Spanish onions, peeled and finely sliced
4 Granny Smith apples
a large bunch of flatleaf parsley, chopped

1 Make the dressing for the slaw by combining all the ingredients in a bowl. Taste for seasoning. To plump up the raisins, leave to soak in a bowl of warm apple juice or water.

2 To make the slaw, put the cabbage in a large mixing bowl with the onions. Peel the apples and slice thinly to the core. Stack the slices and cut again to make very thin matchsticks. Add these to the cabbage and the onion. Then add the chopped parsley and soaked golden raisins.

3 Toss the slaw in the crème fraîche dressing and serve at room temperature.

AN EASY TART

30

TOTAL

Preparation 15

Cooking 15

Serves 4

as a main course or
6–8 as a light snack

**Ready-rolled puff
pastry is great to
keep in the freezer
for any entertaining
emergencies
and is also easy
to pick up from
the refrigerated
section of your
supermarket.**

Ready-rolled puff pastry is an ingredient that I couldn't do without. You can top it with anything you happen to have lying around and you've got a great little dinner. Shop-bought pesto and tapenades are fantastic, baked in the oven with some mozzarella and then topped with basil leaves. I thought I'd go one step further with this recipe – I love this salty combination.

**1 sheet ready-rolled puff pastry measuring
20–30cm in length
1 portion chermoula (see page 48) or a jar
of shop-bought pesto
8 marinated anchovies, cut in half
lengthways**

**2 tablespoons capers
2 tablespoons black olives
200g mozzarella cheese
2 tablespoons olive oil
1 egg, beaten
a small handful of basil leaves**

1 Preheat the oven to 220°C/425°F/Gas 7. Lightly oil a large non-stick baking tray. Lay out the puff pastry on the tray. Score a border 2cm in from the edges of the pastry. This will allow the border to rise and crisp while the middle stays flat.

2 Spread the chermoula over the inner section of the tart and criss-cross the anchovies over the top. Scatter over the capers and olives and then tear over the mozzarella. Drizzle over the olive oil and brush the border with the beaten egg.

3 Put in the hot oven for 10–15 minutes or until the border rises and is golden brown. Remove from the oven and sprinkle over the basil leaves. Cut into pieces on a big board to put in the middle of the table so that everyone can help themselves.

DEEP-FRIED MOZZARELLA BALLS WITH JALAPEÑO CHEESE DIP

25

TOTAL

Preparation 15

Cooking 10

Serves 6

These are the ultimate friendly accompaniment to a cold beer or a classic frozen margarita (see page 172). I don't think any of your friends will be disappointed when served these spicy molten snacks.

For the sauce
200g cream cheese
100ml white wine or water
2 tablespoons jalapeño chillies (from a jar), chopped
4–5 splashes of Tabasco sauce
4–5 splashes of Worcestershire sauce
100g Cheddar cheese, grated

For the mozzarella balls
100g plain flour
150g dried breadcrumbs
3 large eggs
1 litre vegetable oil, for deep-frying
30 bocconcini (tiny mozzarella balls)
salt

1 To make the sauce, put the cream cheese in a saucepan with the wine or water on a medium heat. Add the jalapeños and Tabasco and Worcestershire sauces. Gradually stir in the Cheddar cheese until it has all melted. Keep warm while you make the mozzarella balls.

2 For the mozzarella balls, put the flour and breadcrumbs in separate bowls and beat the eggs in a third. Pour the oil into a shallow, wide-based saucepan (don't fill it more than halfway) and put on a medium heat.

3 Drain and dry the bocconcini and coat first in the flour, then in the beaten egg and finally in the breadcrumbs. Then pass through the egg and breadcrumbs once again to make sure they are coated really well.

4 Test the oil to see if it's hot enough by dropping in a pinch of breadcrumbs. If they bubble and rise to the top, the oil is ready. Gently lower around 6–8 balls at a time into the oil using a slotted spoon and fry for about 1 minute until golden brown. Remove from the oil (again using the slotted spoon) and leave to drain on kitchen paper before sprinkling with salt.

5 Serve the mozzarella balls with the warm dip.

Perfect served with a few beers for friends or as a starter to the Mexican Beef Burritos (see page 139).

CRISPY FRIED SALT AND PEPPER SQUID WITH THAI DIPPING SAUCE

20
TOTAL

Preparation 15
Cooking 5
Serves 4
as a starter

Squid is really cheap and very easily sourced. Try to buy the baby ones with the tentacles tucked inside them as they give a bit of interest to the dish. They are usually already cleaned, so all you have to do is heat up your oil and prepare the batter.

500ml vegetable oil, for deep-frying
12 whole baby squid, cleaned
1 teaspoon baking powder
4 tablespoons plain flour
2 tablespoons cornflour
salt and freshly ground black pepper
100–125ml sparkling water

For the Thai dipping sauce
1 tablespoon Thai fish sauce

1 teaspoon caster sugar
juice of 2 limes
1 green chilli, chopped
2 spring onions, trimmed and finely chopped

To serve
a small handful of coriander, torn
1 lime, cut into wedges

1 Take a large heavy-based saucepan and pour in the vegetable oil. Turn the heat to medium and allow the oil to heat up while you prepare the rest of the dish. If using a deep-fat fryer heat it to 170°C.

2 To prepare the squid, pull the tentacles out of the body. Cut off and discard the sack just above the start of the tentacles. Reserve the tentacles and cut the body into three strips. Dry all the bits well on absorbent kitchen paper.

3 To make the batter, combine the baking powder, flour, cornflour, salt and pepper in a bowl and whisk in the sparkling water. It should be the consistency of a thin yogurt.

4 To make the dipping sauce, combine the Thai fish sauce with the sugar and lime juice and mix well until the sugar has dissolved. Taste to check the balance – it should be not too sweet, nor too salty. Then add the chilli and spring onions.

5 Check the oil is hot enough by dropping a pea-sized drop of the batter into the oil. If it fizzles and bubbles, the oil is at the right temperature. Make sure you have absorbent kitchen paper and a slotted spoon to hand to remove the squid from the oil.

6 Coat the squid pieces in the batter and transfer to the hot oil with the slotted spoon, making sure you lay the squid away from you to avoid burns. Allow the squid to bubble for 2–3 minutes until it is golden brown. Remove from the oil, drain on kitchen paper and serve straight away with the dip, some torn fresh coriander and the lime wedges.

This makes a great starter, follow with Rump Steak with Blue Cheese Butter (see page 88) or Prawn and Egg Fried Rice (see page 46).

SWEETCORN AND SPRING ONION FRITTERS

30
TOTAL

Preparation 15
Cooking 15
Makes 12–15
small fritters

Serve with the
Barbecue Chinese
Ribs (see page 118).

These are a great snack or side dish. They are very easy to cook and use ingredients that would generally be hanging around in your cupboard or fridge. Dip them in guacamole or tomato salsa or eat with sweet chilli sauce.

8 tablespoons self-raising flour
1 teaspoon baking powder
salt and freshly ground black pepper
2 large eggs
325ml milk
2 x 200g tins sweetcorn, drained
3 spring onions, trimmed and sliced

a small bunch of coriander, roughly
    chopped
1 red chilli, chopped
2 tablespoons vegetable oil
guacamole, tomato salsa or sweet chilli
    sauce, to serve (optional)

1 Mix the flour and baking powder in a bowl. Add the salt and pepper and make a well in the centre of the flour. Crack the eggs into the well and whisk together to form a paste. Gradually add the milk, continually whisking, until you have a thick dropping consistency.

2 Add the sweetcorn, spring onions, coriander and chilli to the batter. If it now looks a little thick, add a drop more milk. The batter needs to be able to hold its shape when poured into the pan to cook, so shouldn't be too thin.

3 Heat a frying pan and add the vegetable oil. When the oil is hot, take a tablespoon of the mixture and drop it into the pan. Depending on the size of your pan you should be able to fit four fritters in at once. Cook for about 1½ minutes until golden brown and then flip them over. Cook for a further 2 minutes on the other side and serve.

MEXICAN BEEF BURRITOS WITH CHUNKY GUACAMOLE

45

TOTAL

Preparation 20

Cooking 25

Serves 4

or 6 as a light snack

Spicy Mexican is always great food to tuck in to when you are socialising with friends. The dish is all self-assembled so all you have to do is put the bowls in the middle of the table and let everyone dig in.

2 tablespoons vegetable oil

1 large red onion, peeled and finely chopped

2–3 red chillies, finely chopped (with the seeds in if you're brave enough)

4 garlic cloves, peeled and chopped

2 teaspoons ground cumin

1 teaspoon ground coriander

800g lean minced beef

1 tablespoon tomato purée

salt and freshly ground black pepper

250ml beef stock

1 x 400g tin whole plum tomatoes

a pinch of sugar

1 x 400g tin kidney beans, drained

For the guacamole

2 avocados

1 garlic clove, peeled and grated

1 red chilli, finely chopped

zest of 2 limes

½ bunch of coriander, roughly chopped

½ teaspoon ground cumin

1 tablespoon olive oil

To serve

tomato salsa

soft flour tortillas

soured cream

grated Montgomery Jack, mozzarella or Cheddar cheese

sliced jalapeño peppers

1 To make the chilli filling for the burritos, heat the oil in a large frying pan or casserole dish. Add the onion, chillies and garlic and allow to soften for 5–6 minutes. Then add the cumin and coriander before increasing the heat and adding the minced beef. Try to get a little colour on it, moving everything around in the pan to combine well.

2 Add the tomato purée, season with salt and pepper then add the stock, tomatoes and sugar and cook for 15–20 minutes while you make the guacamole. Reduce the heat so the bottom won't burn and add the kidney beans. Add a bit of water if it looks like it's drying out too much, but be careful as you don't want it sloppy.

3 To make the guacamole, cut the avocados in half, remove the stone and scoop out the flesh using a spoon. Add the garlic, red chilli and lime zest. Using the back of a fork, squash the avocado until you get a chunky purée. Then add the fresh coriander and ground cumin, season well and add the olive oil. Stir and leave until you are ready to serve. This can also be done in a blender if you prefer.

4 Serve the mince with warmed tortillas, the guacamole, salsa, soured cream, grated cheese and some jalapeño peppers.

Have a look through the recipe before you start cooking. Most of the chopping can be done in one go. For example, all the chillies, garlic and onions can be chopped at once to save you doing the job two or three times for different parts of the recipe.

CHICKEN, LEEK AND BACON PIE

55
TOTAL

Preparation 15
Cooking 40
Serves 6

It's nice to make individaul pies as in the picture opposite, but it works just as well making one large one.

A warm and homely pie, this one is perfect for the whole family but made in half the time of a usual pie thanks to the ready-rolled puff pastry.

200g smoked lardons or smoked bacon
  rashers, chopped
500g chicken thighs, diced
2 bay leaves
salt and freshly ground black pepper
50g butter

3 leeks, trimmed and sliced
3 tablespoons plain flour
500ml chicken stock
1 sheet ready-rolled puff pastry
1 egg, beaten

1 Preheat the oven to 200°C/400°F/Gas 6. Place a large saucepan on the stove on a medium heat and add the lardons or chopped bacon. When this has started to crisp and go golden brown, add the chicken and bay leaves. Season with salt and pepper.

2 Add the butter and leeks to the pan, cover, and let the leeks cook for 3–5 minutes until wilted. Add the flour and stir well and then pour in the chicken stock. Stir well while the mixture comes to the boil. Remove from the heat and pour the mixture into a pie or casserole dish. Make sure you choose a dish or individual dishes that the puff pastry will cover. If using individual dishes you may need 2 sheets of pastry.

3 Cut a strip of the pre-rolled pastry and mould the strip around the rim of the pie dish. Brush this with beaten egg and lay the remaining pastry on top. Press down around the rim well and trim off any excess. Make a small hole in the top of the pastry, brush well with beaten egg and sprinkle with salt.

4 Put the pie in the oven for about 30 minutes or until golden brown. Serve immediately.

Sweet Tooth

There are odd occasions when we all need a little sweet something. It might be a sneaky piece of chocolate or a big bowl of berries. Whatever tickles your fancy, it's always good to have a choice. In this chapter I have created simple desserts that can be cooked in minutes. No setting times or hours of baking involved. These dishes will only take a few minutes out of your busy day to make something comforting and sweet to perfectly finish off a meal. Some recipes may take a bit longer than others, but none are overly complicated. Whatever your pudding requirements are, I'm sure you will find something in here to satisfy yourself, friends, kids and family.

BAKED APRICOT BRIOCHE

This dessert works really well with fresh fruits such as pears, peaches and nectarines, especially when ripe and in season.

This dish is a quick take on the much-loved bread and butter pudding, but without the cooking and setting time. It's no harder to prepare than making a quick sandwich.

1 small brioche loaf or 3 large croissants
50g softened unsalted butter
100g apricot jam

2 x 400g tins halved apricots in juice
100g golden caster sugar
vanilla ice cream or double cream, to serve

1 Preheat the oven to 200°C/400°F/Gas 6. Slice the brioche loaf into six thick slices or the croissants in half lengthways and butter on both sides. Lay the slices in an ovenproof dish roughly measuring 20 x 20cm (you may need another brioche loaf to cover the bottom of the dish) and generously spread over the apricot jam.

2 Drain the apricots (reserving some of the juice) and lay cut-side down onto the buttered and jammed brioche. Sprinkle the sugar over the top and drizzle with 2–3 tablespoons of the reserved apricot juice.

3 Bake in the oven for 10–15 minutes or until slightly crispy at the edges. Serve with the accompaniment of your choice.

ALMOND, HAZELNUT AND VANILLA BUTTER BISCUITS

20

TOTAL

Preparation 5
Cooking 15
Makes 12–14
biscuits

You can freeze this dough in greaseproof paper to have on standby.

If you don't fancy making a dessert when entertaining on a weeknight, but feel you should satisfy that sweet tooth at the end of a meal, I have the perfect solution. Biscuits served with a strong shot of espresso really hit the spot. Warm, freshly cooked biscuits are a very special treat and a really elegant way to finish off a meal.

150g unsalted butter
100g caster sugar
100g plain flour

½ vanilla pod, seeds scraped from the pod
100g ground almonds
50g hazelnuts, lightly smashed

1 Preheat the oven to 180°C/350°F/Gas 4. Cream the butter and sugar together either in a blender or by hand until smooth and well combined. Fold in the flour, vanilla seeds and almonds and combine well. Scatter in the hazelnuts.

2 Divide the mixture into 12–14 balls and place on a lined non-stick baking tray, making sure they are not too close together. Bake in the oven for 15 minutes until golden brown. Leave to cool for a few minutes before serving. The biscuits will keep for a week in an airtight container.

BERRY GRATIN

20
TOTAL

Preparation 15
Cooking 5
Serves 6

This is such a lovely simple recipe and has a definite touch of class. Summery and colourful, it's a special way to finish off a meal.

250ml double cream
1 teaspoon vanilla paste or 1 vanilla pod
4 eggs, separated
150g caster sugar
1 tablespoon cornflour

splash of rum or Grand Marnier (optional)
500g mixed summer berries, such as
    strawberries, blueberries, raspberries and
    blackberries

1 Heat the double cream in a saucepan on a low heat with the vanilla paste or cut the vanilla pod in half lengthways and scrape out the seeds with a small knife into the pan and add pods to infuse too. Don't allow it to come to the boil.

2 In another saucepan, whisk together the egg yolks, sugar and cornflour and slowly pour the hot cream over the mixture. Place the pan over a low heat and stir continuously for 5–6 minutes or until the custard thickens to the consistency of thin yogurt. Don't leave the custard on the stove without stirring or you will end up with scrambled eggs. Once thickened, remove from the heat. Add a splash of the rum or Grand Marnier at this stage, if you wish.

3 Preheat the grill to medium. Scatter the mixed berries in the bottom of either individual heatproof bowls or one large baking dish.

4 Whisk the egg whites with a hand-held electric whisk until firm peaks start to form and carefully fold into the thickened custard. Pour the mixture over the berries and place under the grill for 1–2 minutes until an even golden brown. Serve warm.

Don't worry about having matching ramekins for this. I always think it's quite nice to have a bit of mix and match.

THE DREADED SOUFFLÉ (LEMON FLAVOUR)

I can totally understand why people are so scared of soufflés. There are horror stories of them not rising, sinking and exploding. My view is if you don't try, you'll never know. I've made imperfect soufflés in my time, but I'm not sure that anyone has ever really noticed at a dinner party. As long as they are light and fluffy, who cares what shape they are? This one is very easy, so please don't worry about it.

20g unsalted butter
50g caster sugar, plus 2 teaspoons
2 large eggs, separated

2 tablespoons lemon curd
zest of 2 lemons
icing sugar, to serve

1 Preheat the oven to 200°C/400°F/Gas 6. Melt the butter in a small saucepan. Brush two small ramekins in an upward motion with the butter using a pastry brush. Put 1 teaspoon of sugar in each ramekin and roll it around so the inside is coated in sugar. Put them in the fridge.

2 Mix the egg yolks well with the lemon curd and the lemon zest in a large mixing bowl. In a separate clean and dry bowl, whisk the whites using an electric whisk until stiff peaks start to form. Then, still whisking, slowly start adding the sugar. When the whites are at firm peaks (so they stand on their own without flopping over), stop whisking. Gently fold one large spoon of the whisked whites into the yolk and lemon curd mixture. Use a metal spoon to do this, then gradually add the rest until all the whites are folded into the yolks. Do this slowly and don't overwork the mixture.

3 Spoon the mixture into the buttered and sugared ramekins. Gently tap the ramekins on the work surface so any bubbles rise to the top, and smooth out the mixture with a spatula. Bake in the oven for about 10 minutes until well risen. Try not to open the door while they are cooking. Remove from the oven and sprinkle with icing sugar before serving immediately.

20
TOTAL

Preparation 10
Cooking 10
Serves 2

Try replacing the lemon curd with Nutella and a crushed ripe banana for a different twist.

AN EASY MESS

10
—
TOTAL

Preparation 10
Cooking 0
Serves 4

This is a classic recipe that never fails. However, the downside used to be that you would have had to wait three hours while you make the perfect crispy meringue, something that very few of us have time do to during the week while working. Thanks to our wonderfully stocked supermarkets, however, we cooks now have a solution... ready-made meringues. Now we can all make a mess with ease!

1 large ready-made meringue nest
200g mascarpone cheese
75g icing sugar
100g crème fraîche
1 vanilla pod, cut in half lengthways and the seeds scraped out or 1 teaspoon vanilla bean paste
juice of ½ lemon

300g fresh strawberries
200g fresh raspberries
4 scoops of vanilla or raspberry ripple ice cream

For the coulis
300g fresh raspberries
1 tablespoon icing sugar

1 Put the meringue into a plastic sandwich bag and bash lightly using a rolling pin or similar heavy object.

2 Put the mascarpone in a bowl and stir well to loosen. Mix in the icing sugar together with the crème fraîche, vanilla seeds and lemon juice. Hull the strawberries and cut into small pieces. Fold these through the sweetened cream together with the raspberries.

3 Make the coulis by pushing the raspberries though a fine sieve using the back of a spoon. Discard the pips and sweeten the purée to taste with the icing sugar.

4 When you are ready to serve, fold the crushed meringues through the strawberry and raspberry cream. Put a scoop of your chosen ice cream in the base of your serving glass, drizzle over a little of the coulis and pile on the cream. Drizzle with a final teaspoon of coulis before serving.

You can use all sorts of fruit for this depending on what's in season. Stewed plums with a pinch of cinnamon work particularly well.

BLUEBERRY PIE

40

TOTAL

Preparation 10
Cooking 30
Serves 6

Thanks to the convenient invention of ready-rolled pastry, we no longer need to spend all our time crumbling, kneading, resting and rolling the top for a lovely berry pie. The filling for this pie is simple and has great flavour as the berries burst their juices when you bite into them. Accompanied by a crispy, sugary topping and cold ice cream, this pudding is the perfect way end to a meal.

juice of 2 lemons
6 tablespoons caster sugar
100g unsalted butter
1 tablespoon cornflour
500g blueberries
clotted cream or vanilla ice cream, to serve

For the pastry
1 sheet ready-rolled sweetcrust pastry
1 egg, beaten
a sprinkling of brown sugar
a pinch of ground cinnamon

1 Preheat the oven to 200°C/400°F/Gas 6. Make the filling by combining the lemon juice with the sugar in a small saucepan heating gently. Add the butter and the cornflour and mix to a smooth paste. Then add the blueberries and mix thoroughly.

2 Cut a thin strip off the edge of the pre-rolled pastry and stick this around the edge of a 500ml pie dish using your thumb to press it to the rim. Pour the blueberries into the dish.

3 Paint the beaten egg around the pastry rim and lay over the remaining pastry. Seal the edges using either your thumb or a fork and trim off any excess pastry. Make a small hole in the top for steam to escape and paint more egg wash over the top. Sprinkle with the sugar and cinnamon and bake in the oven for about 30 minutes until the top is golden brown and crisp.

4 Serve either with clotted cream or vanilla ice cream.

Serve after the Rump Steak with Blue Cheese Butter (see page 88).

CHOCOLATE AND ORANGE YORKIES

20–22
TOTAL

Preparation 10
Cooking 10–12
Serves 6

Try using white chocolate and raspberries for an alternative.

I assume that most of us have a vague idea of how to throw together a simple Yorkshire pudding batter mix – hardly any measuring is needed. So why not do exactly the same, but add sugar and make it a sweet version? Of course, I had to add a few other little bits and pieces to make it even more inviting and tempting.... but that's my job. I promise this is no different to a Yorkshire pudding batter, you just eat it after the main meal instead of with it.

6 teaspoons vegetable oil
225g plain flour
3 tablespoons caster sugar
1 teaspoon baking powder
zest of 2 oranges

3 eggs, lightly beaten
250ml semi-skimmed milk
½ teaspoon vanilla extract
100g chocolate buttons
double cream, to serve

1 Preheat the oven to 220°C/425°F/Gas 7. Pour half a teaspoon of vegetable oil into each hole in a 12-hole muffin tin and place in the oven to heat up.

2 Put the flour into a bowl with the sugar, baking powder and orange zest. Make a well in the centre of the flour and pour in the eggs. Beat together with a whisk before slowly adding the milk and then mix in the vanilla extract.

3 Remove the muffin tin carefully from the oven and pour an equal amount of the batter into each one. Drop 4–5 chocolate buttons into each muffin hole and bake in the oven for 10–12 minutes, until risen and golden brown. Serve while hot with the double cream.

BANANA PUDDING WITH TOFFEE SAUCE

20
TOTAL

Preparation 10
Cooking 10
Serves 4–6

I love the word pudding, although I'm not entirely sure what it means. Dessert? Cake? Whatever it is, this particular recipe just about sums up the word to me and I promise, even if people say they don't want dessert, they will when you bring this one out and put it on the table. You don't even have to get more than one bowl dirty. A whisk and a baking dish is all you need for the pudding, plus a saucepan for the sauce. How much easier can you get?

100g softened unsalted butter, plus more
  for greasing
3 ripe bananas
100g plain flour
1 teaspoon baking powder
1 teaspoon ground cinnamon
100g light brown sugar
a pinch of salt

1 teaspoon vanilla paste or extract
2 eggs, beaten
2 tablespoons milk

For the toffee sauce
75g light brown sugar
75g butter
100ml double cream

1 Grease a 1 litre baking dish (make sure it fits in your microwave) with butter. Add the remaining butter to the dish and microwave on a medium setting for 30 seconds until the butter has melted. Keep your eye on it as you don't want it to explode and make a mess.

2 Peel two of the bananas and squash them into the melted butter using the back of a fork. Add the flour, baking powder, cinnamon, sugar, salt and vanilla and mix well with a wooden spoon. Then add the eggs and milk and combine to form a paste. Gently tap the dish on the work surface to even out the mixture and slice the remaining banana on top. Cover with clingfilm and put in the microwave. Cook on a high heat for 8 minutes.

3 Meanwhile, make the sauce by boiling the sugar and butter for 3–4 minutes, then add the cream. Allow the sauce to bubble and serve with the banana pudding.

If you're really pushed for time serve with vanilla ice cream instead of the toffee sauce.

PINEAPPLE KEBABS WITH VANILLA AND MAPLE SYRUP

20

TOTAL

Preparation 10
Cooking 10
Serves 4–6

This is great cooked on the barbecue if the weather is nice.

This is a really straightforward dessert and hot pineapple with cold ice cream and sweet syrup is something very special. This recipe is also great with banana.

1 supersweet medium-sized pineapple or 2–3 packets of pineapple, pre-cut into chunks

1 teaspoon vanilla paste or 1 vanilla pod
6 tablespoons maple syrup
vanilla ice cream, to serve

1 Preheat a griddle pan or large frying pan on a medium heat. If you have bought a whole fresh pineapple, you will need to top and tail it. Remove the spiky outer skin using a serrated knife, trying to remove the eyes (brown spots) on the flesh as you go. Cut the pineapple in half, and then cut each half into 4–6 strips. Remove the middle woody core. Push the pineapple strip onto wooden or metal skewers. If you have bought pre-cut pineapple it will be in chunks so push 5–6 pieces onto each skewer.

2 In a saucepan, mix the vanilla paste or seeds (removed from the pod using a small knife) with the maple syrup and gently heat to a simmer. Brush the syrup onto the pineapple skewers. Lay onto the hot griddle and cook until they start to caramelise. Turn in the pan to ensure they cook and colour evenly. Brush with the syrup as you go. This can also be done under the grill, but you must soak the skewers if you are using wooden ones or they will burn.

3 Remove from the pan, pour over the remaining syrup and serve with ice cream.

PEACH AND PISTACHIO TRIFLE

15
TOTAL

Preparation 15
Cooking 0
Serves 6

It's really important to keep your cupboard stocked up with the basics and tinned peaches, apricots and pears are all useful essentials. When not in season these tinned fruits have a great texture, flavour and sweetness to liven up a quick dessert.

200ml double cream
200g mascarpone cheese
zest and juice of 1 large orange
½ teaspoon vanilla extract or paste
125g icing sugar
2 x 400g tins halved peaches in juice
2 tablespoons Madeira wine or sweet
   sherry

½ brioche loaf or 1 loaf Madeira cake,
   cut into 1cm-thick slices
100g pistachio nuts, shelled and peeled if
   possible, roughly chopped
a small handful of mint leaves
2 tablespoons runny honey

1 Whip the double cream in a large bowl until soft peaks form. In a separate bowl, beat the mascarpone and fold it into the double cream. Add in the orange zest and juice, vanilla extract or paste and sift in the icing sugar. Stir to mix.

2 Drain the peaches and reserve the juice. Pour the juice into a bowl and add the Madeira or sweet sherry. Add 2 tablespoons of the sherry-flavoured peach juice to the cream mixture and beat well.

3 Slice by slice, dip the brioche or Madeira cake into the flavoured peach juice, just long enough to coat the cake, but not allowing it to go soggy. Lay each slice in the bottom of a serving dish until all the gaps are filled on the base.

4 Lay the drained peaches on top of the cake and then generously spoon on the sweetened cream up to the rim of the dish. Sprinkle on the chopped pistachios, tear over the mint leaves and drizzle with the runny honey. Serve immediately.

Peeled pistachios are available from most Turkish supermarkets if you have difficulty finding them elsewhere.

RICOTTA AND RASPBERRY FRITTERS WITH CINNAMON

20–25
TOTAL

Preparation 10
Cooking 10–15
Serves 6

Oh so easy to prepare and far too easy to eat! A great dessert for finger food at the end of a big tuck-in dinner. You must try these – trust me, you'll wish you made more of the mixture, once the first batch has been devoured.

500ml vegetable oil, for deep-frying
250g ricotta
1 egg
2 egg yolks
6 tablespoons plain flour

2 level teaspoons baking powder
1½ teaspoons ground cinnamon
5 tablespoons caster sugar
150g fresh raspberries

1 Put enough oil into a wide, deep frying pan so it's about 5cm deep, but not more than half-way full. Heat the oil to 170°C on a medium heat. If you have a deep-fat fryer heat to 170°C.

2 Put the ricotta into a bowl and add the egg, egg yolks, flour, baking powder, ½ teaspoon of the cinnamon and 2 tablespoons of the caster sugar. Using a hand-held electric whisk, beat the mixture until smooth. Gently fold in the raspberries. Mix the remaining caster sugar and cinnamon together in a shallow dish and set aside for later.

3 Check to see if the oil is at the right temperature by dropping in a pea-sized drop of the mixture. If it sizzles in the oil, you know it's hot enough. Get ready to fry by making sure you have a slotted spoon and kitchen paper to drain the oil off the fritters once cooked.

4 Using a tablespoon, take a spoonful of the mixture (try to get one raspberry per spoonful) and drop it carefully into the hot oil. Use another spoon to push the mixture off the spoon if you need to. Don't put too many into the pan at once. Fry each fritter for about 3–4 minutes until golden brown, turning once or twice in the oil to make sure the colour is even. They will puff up and expand while cooking.

5 Remove the cooked fritters from the oil with a slotted spoon and place on kitchen paper to drain. Once all the fritters are fried, roll them in the sugar and cinnamon mixture and serve immediately while still hot.

Turn off the oil and leave it to cool completely before discarding.

TIRAMISU

You can make this in advance as it will keep for a few days in the fridge. Just re-dust with cocoa before you serve.

This is still one of my all-time favourite desserts and it's so easy to prepare. I make this at nearly every dinner party and I'm sure my guests are getting bored of it by now, but I just can't help it.

3 eggs, separated
1 teaspoon vanilla paste
8 tablespoons icing sugar
zest of 1 lemon
1 shot Madeira wine (or any fortified wine)

500g mascarpone cheese
16 Amaretti biscuits
50ml espresso or very strong coffee
cocoa powder, to serve

1 Whisk the egg yolks together with the vanilla paste, icing sugar, lemon zest and Madeira with an electric hand-held whisk until pale. When pale, add the mascarpone cheese and whisk again.

2 In a separate clean and dry bowl, whisk the whites using an electric whisk (with clean beaters) until stiff peaks start to form. Fold into the mascarpone mixture.

3 Soak the Amaretti biscuits in the coffee and lay two in the bottom of each serving glass. Spoon a generous amount of mascarpone cream on top of each one and dust with cocoa powder. Soak the remaining biscuits in the coffee and put on top of the mascarpone cream. Evenly distribute the remaining cream and smooth over the top. Dust with cocoa as you are about to serve.

VANILLA RICE PUDDING WITH BLUEBERRY COMPOTE

25

TOTAL

Preparation 5
Cooking 20
Serves 6–8

Use a spoonful or two of your favourite jam instead of a fruit compote for a quick cheat.

I love rice pudding, but I really don't like it when it's baked in the oven. So, I always cook rice pudding as I would a risotto and serve it with something fruity – blueberries, in this case, but rhubarb, raspberry, strawberry or peach will also do nicely.

750ml semi-skimmed milk
1 teaspoon vanilla paste or vanilla pod,
   split in half lengthways
170g caster sugar
300g pudding rice or risotto rice
100ml double cream

For the compote
400g fresh or frozen blueberries
zest and juice of 1 large orange
4 tablespoons caster sugar
a pinch of ground cinnamon
25g unsalted butter

1 Pour the milk into a saucepan and add the vanilla paste or vanilla pod and the sugar. Add the rice and bring to the boil. Reduce the heat and let the rice simmer. Mix every 2–3 minutes until the rice is cooked.

2 Meanwhile, make the blueberry compote. Put the blueberries into a saucepan (if using frozen there is no need to defrost first) and add the orange zest and juice, sugar, cinnamon and butter with 2 tablespoons of water. Cook on a low heat for about 10 minutes until soft.

3 Once the rice is cooked and the milk absorbed, pour in the double cream and pull out the vanilla pod. Heat through again, spoon the pudding into bowls and serve with a spoonful of the compote.

Fancy a Drink?

If I am entertaining or celebrating a special occasion, cocktails are always on the must list. A few of the recipes in this book have been created to make your life while entertaining that little bit easier and that should not stop with food. Cocktails always make a party or any social event go with a swing but making them can often be quite time consuming. I want to show you my cheat ways of getting around all that Boston shaking and muddling of the mojitos. All these drinks can sit happily in a jug in the fridge and then be finished over crushed ice or with a splash of something fizzy.

PEACH BELLINI

5

TOTAL

Preparation 5
Makes 10–12
cocktails

**Peach purée
is available
in most
supermarkets
in the drinks
section or in
the desserts
section.**

This is a bit of a cheat, but I find that it's the best Bellini. It's easy to make and perfect for a busy party.

1 x 400g tin peaches or 200ml peach purée

**100ml vodka
2 bottles Prosecco, to serve**

1 Put the tinned peaches with their syrup and the vodka into a food-processor. Whizz to a purée and then keep in a jug or squeezy bottle until ready to serve. If using peach purée, mix the purée with the vodka and set aside.

2 When ready, put a small amount of the peach purée at the bottom of a champagne glass. Tilt the glass very slightly and pour the Prosecco down the side of the glass trying to create a layer. You can also pour it down the back of a teaspoon. Serve while the bubbles are still fizzing and add a stirrer for presentation if you wish.

A CLASSIC COSMO

5

TOTAL

Preparation 5
plus chilling time
Makes 8–10
martini-size
glasses

This is the best cocktail to put in the freezer and leave to chill. It saves shaking it over ice every time you get another request from a guest and – trust me – you will.

**450ml vodka
300ml cranberry juice
150ml Cointreau**

**75ml fresh lime juice
strips of orange zest, to serve**

Mix all the ingredients in a large jug. Chill in the freezer and then, once it is really ice cold, move to the fridge.

CHILLI AND GINGER MOJITO

10

TOTAL

Preparation 10

Makes 8

cocktails

This is a mojito that is guaranteed to give a little kick. You don't want to make it so spicy that it blows your head off, you just want a little twinge at the back of your throat that tells you you've just had chilli. The ginger freshens the drink up really nicely and goes so well with the classic minty rum-based cocktail.

3 large red chillies, deseeded and cut into
fine strips
10cm piece of fresh ginger, peeled and cut
into fine strips
10 brown sugar cubes
6 limes, cut into eighths

2 large handfuls of mint leaves
crushed ice
8 tablespoons gomme (sugar syrup)
500ml golden spiced rum
400ml apple juice (optional)

1 Put the chilli and ginger in a bowl with the sugar, lime and mint. Using the end of a rolling pin, crush all the ingredients together well. (You can also do this with a pestle and mortar.) Leave this covered in the fridge until the party starts.

2 When your guests arrive, spoon out a tablespoon of the mint and lime mixture into each glass and add the crushed ice. Add 1 tablespoon of gomme to each cocktail and mix this around before topping up with golden rum. I usually add a splash of apple juice to sweeten it up a bit (and make it a bit less lethal).

RUM PUNCH

5

TOTAL

Preparation 5

plus chilling time

Makes 12

cocktails

I learned this cocktail while working in Tobago last year. My clients loved a pitcher of this delicious drink before heading out for the night, and I must say that I became rather partial to a small glass myself. It's fruity and fresh, not to mention dangerous as you don't realise just how strong it is.

100ml fresh lime juice
200ml grenadine syrup
300ml golden rum

200ml pineapple juice
200ml grapefruit juice
10 splashes Angostura bitters

Mix in a large jug or individual glasses, chill and serve with ice!

THE TOM PEPPER

5
TOTAL

Preparation 5
plus chilling time

Makes 8
cocktails

Oh no, egos are going to grow! Huge thanks to Jason Capper for the recipe and to Tom ... for everything!

400ml vodka
200ml puréed strawberries
120ml berry liqueur
120ml lemon juice
200ml sparkling wine

To serve
sliced strawberries
black pepper

1 Mix all the ingredients in a jug and chill in the fridge until needed.

2 When ready to serve, pour over crushed ice in individual glasses and top with sparkling wine. Finish with strawberry slices and cracked black pepper.

A CLASSIC MARGARITA

5
TOTAL

Preparation 5
plus chilling time

Makes 10–12
cocktails

It's impossible to eat Mexican food with friends without a pitcher of frozen margaritas. I know you are meant to roll the edge of the glass in salt, but I'm not such a fan of this so I do fifty/fifty – half sugar, half salt. It's sensible to go for a good tequila, or you'll feel it the next day.

1.2 litres tequila
600ml Cointreau
300ml fresh lime juice
crushed ice

3 tablespoons salt
3 tablespoons caster sugar
1 lime, cut into 8 slices, to garnish

1 To prepare the cocktail in advance, mix the tequila, Cointreau and lime juice together and leave in the fridge. This can be drunk as it is, but I like mine frozen.

2 When you're ready to serve, put the ice into a blender and add the margarita mixture. Mix the salt and sugar in a bowl and rub lime juice around the rim of each glass. Dip the glasses into the salt and sugar mixture, pour out the frozen margaritas and serve.

30—60
MINUTE MEALS INDEX

INGREDIENTS INDEX